D0622292

From Geography to Geotechnics

University of Illinois Press   Urbana · Chicago · London   1968

FROM GEOGRAPHY TO GEOTECHNICS

by **Benton MacKaye**
Edited by Paul T. Bryant

G L Copa

252 78415 4

Contents

Introduction

by Paul T. Bryant

Man in the landscape, what might be called ecological humanism, has been the focus of Benton MacKaye's writing and thought over a long and prolific career. Since his first published essay, in the *Journal of the New York State Forestry Association* in 1916, MacKaye has published more than 60 articles in magazines and journals as widely divergent as the *Southern Lumberman* and *The New Republic*. These are in addition to his book, *The New Exploration,* countless newspaper articles and letters to editors, and bulletins and reports for such public agencies as the U. S. Forest Service and the Tennessee Valley Authority. From this body of writing, the essays in this volume have been selected as representative works of continuing interest to planners, scholars, conservationists, and private citizens concerned about the effects of our urbanized and deteriorating environment on the quality of our lives.

Lewis Mumford puts MacKaye in the same tradition with Henry David Thoreau and George Perkins Marsh, a tradition that also includes John Burroughs, Frederick Law Olmstead, John Muir, and others aware of the interaction between man's spirit and his environment. MacKaye's central concept is an Emersonian belief in self-realization through harmony with society and nature.

His writing is an attempt to offer modern society practical means to achieve such harmony.

As an ecological humanist, MacKaye is a visualizer but never merely a visionary. He urges us toward visualized ends in shaping our environment, but he never allows his enthusiasm for the ideal to carry him beyond a consideration of practical means. As a New Englander whose cultural and intellectual roots reach well down into the nineteenth century, MacKaye has maintained the Emersonian view which, even at its most transcendental, still recognizes the existence of nature also as commodity.

MacKaye's visualization helps us see the patterns— and potential patterns—in our man-made urban wilderness. His writings help us understand the relationship between ourselves and our civilization, providing at least a preliminary chart to a balanced and lasting culture. These ideas have grown from MacKaye's own experience of harmony with society and the landscape in a New England hill village, experience ideally suited to the development of insight into the cultural impact of environment.

Benton MacKaye was born in 1879, the son of playwright-producer Steele MacKaye. He grew up in an atmosphere of drama, literature, and high moral earnestness. His brother James, a successful industrial chemist, wrote books on philosophy and taught the subject at Dartmouth after his retirement from industry. His brother Percy was a playwright particularly interested in folk materials. His sister Hazel was a poet and worked to develop the pageant as a means toward cultural awareness of folk traditions.

From this background and a Harvard A.B. (class of 1900), Benton MacKaye found his way to the new profession of forestry (Harvard School of Forestry, A.M., 1905) and the newly established Forest Service under Gifford Pinchot. His early work in making the earth more habitable was the rigorously practical, notably unvisionary task of making woodlots yield a maximum of marketable timber on a sustained basis.

MacKaye's childhood in rural New England was pivotal in his view of the environment. The New England hill village still provided a balanced environment with primeval woods, cultivated fields and orchards, and town. The people in his home town of Shirley Center, Massachusetts, might be merchants or tradesmen or farmers, but they all had a conscious relationship with the land, the community, and each other. Their society was stable and harmonious with the landscape. MacKaye's awareness of the values in this society has not made him a romantic, longing for a nostalgic return to the past, nor does he seek to impose on all times and places a synthetic New England village. On the other hand, it has helped him see the possibilities inherent in such harmony and stability.

During MacKaye's childhood, the last frontiers of the West were closing and the East was industrializing. He grew up when Americans were coming to realize that the West was no longer a wilderness reserve for future development. America was facing the problem of living on the land it had already settled. This realization belatedly opened the way for visualizers, planners, and conservationists like MacKaye.

The consequences of this are explored in the span of MacKaye's work, from the days of Theodore Roosevelt and Gifford Pinchot to the age of the atom and space exploration and the negative "one world" implications of the intercontinental missile. The essays in this collection, taken from that span, fall readily under three headings: "Geography to Geotechnics," "Control of the Landscape," and "Uses for the Wilderness."

The first essay on control of the landscape, "The First

Soldier Colony," harks back to the ending of the frontier and shows the mistakes made in the opening of the western lands, mistakes paid for in hardship, tragedy, waste of resources, and in many cases destruction of a potentially excellent environment by greedy exploitation. Although the great frontier was closed by this time, World War I made analysis of these mistakes pertinent by again raising the possibility of large scale colonization of undeveloped lands.

During the Wilson administration, MacKaye had left the Forest Service and gone to work for the Labor Department under Assistant Secretary Louis Post. As a forester, MacKaye was interested in the problems of agricultural colonization of cut-over "stump" lands left in the upper Mississippi Valley by a rapacious logging industry. Cooperative colonization was MacKaye's central idea, with the government providing the heavy equipment to remove stumps, build roads and houses, and otherwise prepare the area for settlement. MacKaye felt that Robinson Crusoe was not the model for every unemployed mill hand seeking a fresh start. The lone figure in the wilderness seems heroic when he prevails, but masses of settlers moving into a new region should not be confronted with the backbreaking, spirit killing drudgery of grubbing out stumps and building roads by hand, when society had the tools and the technology to do those jobs more efficiently and quickly with heavy machinery. The result of individualistic efforts in settling the West, MacKaye showed, often was a destruction of the environment that led finally to the disintegration of the fledgling society of the new region. He felt that the lesson should be learned and such mistakes not made again.

As the end of World War I neared, Allied governments began seeking ways to absorb demobilized soldiers and sailors into a peacetime economy with a minimum of social and economic dislocation. One possibility that attracted attention in nations that still had empty land— Canada, Australia, New Zealand, the United States—was the promotion of agricultural colonies to open up these new lands. MacKaye became involved in such planning in this country, and in the course of his work he visited such a project at Kapuskasing in Canada. His article describes that colony and the lessons to be learned from it.

MacKaye sees the Kapuskasing venture as lying somewhere between the old, wasteful settlement of the West and a kind of colonization that develops maximum community interests, prevents land speculation, and uses community strength to avoid the dehumanization of attempting individually tasks that can be efficiently done only with large machinery and joint efforts of many people.

At Kapuskasing the government did clear some land and construct houses, but the land was not surveyed and classified. Thus the unwary settler might find himself the unhappy owner of sterile muskeg rather than fertile crop land. Perhaps more serious, settlers were allowed to choose sites at random over a wide area. Most settled along the railroad right-of-way with no thought of community or knowledge of where others might choose their land. Thus instead of "settlements" close together for mutual help and the social benefits of having neighbors, homesteads were scattered for miles along the railroad, making social life difficult if not impossible. Finally, giving the land in fee simple opened the door to speculators.

This is an early instance of the need for reconciling individualism and planning. Government officials and planners alike should have seen that community interests required settlement in some pattern. A viable community composed of individuals in a meaningful relationship with each other as well as with the land would have kept true individuality from being overwhelmed by the drudgery of single combat against the wilderness and the bleakness of isolation. An important part of any man's true nature as an individual, MacKaye would contend, can only be realized through interaction with others.

In the United States, the rush back to "normalcy" that followed the end of World War I precluded any serious effort at colonization, and so MacKaye's proposals remained on paper. Nevertheless, this work helped focus his attention on broader problems of economics, community structure, and social organization. This line of interest led him to participation in the Regional Planning Association of America in the 1920's, and to government projects like the Tennessee Valley Authority in the 1930's and 1940's. The other essays in the "Control of the Landscape" group grew out of this work.

MacKaye's Spenglerian approach to history is suggested in "End or Peak of Civilization?" But as the question mark suggests, he is Spenglerian with a difference. Like Lewis Mumford and others in the Regional Planning Association, MacKaye saw in the development of America the cyclical pattern of rise and fall of a civilization as described by Oswald Spengler. The pattern, as Spengler predicted, has proceeded as far as the final stage: extreme urbanization. But MacKaye has refused to accept this predicted culmination as inevitable. Instead, he has sought an alternative, a way to revitalize our civilization and either begin the cycle again without passing through a "winter" or death stage, or better, to find a stable state of rich cultural development, drawing its being so fully from harmony with society and the landscape that cyclical change will no longer occur. This stability must have a balance, a harmony among men and between man and the land that will enable man to develop his fullest potential.

MacKaye does not ignore the material or the commercial; he touches on the problems of the flow of goods in a civilization out of balance. But his real concern is the four "folk flows" that he describes. The first was of farmer-settlers moving outward into the virgin continent after 1776. Then when steam revolutionized transportation, the directions of this flow along stream courses or uniformly over wide areas was changed from an "outflow" to a reflow, in which settlement was reoriented along the railroads. When the frontiers closed and cities began to grow, there was begun an "inflow" from the rural to urban centers. This in itself MacKaye does not see negatively. True cities that function as organic communities in a harmonious relationship with the surrounding region are essential to a viable culture. It is rather the fourth flow, the one still continuing, that MacKaye believes carries the seeds of death. This, which he calls the "backflow," is the metropolitan invasion, the overflow of population outward from the cities into amorphous, inorganic, nonfunctional suburbs and motor slums.

The true city, the rural, and the primeval MacKaye considers indigenous and vital, aspects of the balanced environment for a culture that has grown out of its own past, its own traditions, its own community of interests, and its own landscape. Indigenous culture is MacKaye's key to breaking the Spenglerian cycle before the stage of winter and death. The indigenous must meet and stop the invasion of the metropolis, the intrusive mass of formless, cultureless, communityless suburb, or our culture is finally doomed.

Just such a victory seemed possible when MacKaye wrote in 1933 about the proposed federal plan for the Tennessee Valley. He saw this indeed as the "seed of a national plan." Here was a practical, direct start on the development of a region *as a region,* an awareness of a river valley as an indigenous unit culturally and economically as well as physiographically. The plan seemed an opportunity to bring what is best of modern civilization to the isolated hill folk. On the other hand it offered a start for a chain of regional plans along the strategically positioned Appalachian range, on the doorstep of the eastern metropolitan invasion. Such regional development would provide a buffer to stop that invasion and an example to encourage genuine regional development even in the urban wilderness of the eastern seaboard. The seaboard was where the metropolitan invasion was most advanced and widespread, and so that was where the counterattack to save our culture would have to begin. Environment, for MacKaye, is the source from which a genuine culture springs. Saving the environment from megalopolis was the beginning of saving the culture from death.

His appeal that we not confuse environment with beauty, because beauty is only a part of the whole, illustrates a common difficulty MacKaye himself had in subsequent years in his work with the TVA. Landscaping along a roadway (as he suggests in a letter to Stuart Chase, "planting a few pansies"), falls far short of MacKaye's visualization of a culture based on the indigenous experience of the region. Architecture and landscaping are significant, but MacKaye's concept of environment goes far deeper.

The brief presentation of the "townless highway" concept in this article is a summary of what he developed at greater length in "The Townless Highway" in the March

12, 1930, issue of *The New Republic.** The concept is based on a realization of the basic difference between automobile and "horse and buggy" traffic. With horses as the motive force, traffic could pass through towns and down main street without any disruption of the community structure or notable hindrance to the traffic. On this basis the custom began of having the main roads go through towns or in some cases the towns grew around the road. But MacKaye and others of the Regional Planning Association had long since seen that the automobile is not really a "horseless carriage." It is a locomotive not restricted to rails. Inter-city traffic, then, could not be expected to blend with the quiet, leisurely local traffic, but would instead cause the same kind of disruption of the community as the routing of a railroad down main street. A corollary of this, of course, is the question of limited access for such "gasoline locomotive" routes, both as a way of speeding traffic flow and as a safety measure. This may seem obvious enough now to those familiar with modern planning techniques, but even after World War II, and occasionally still, we hear the clamor of local business interests for the routing of a highway through the business district.

Beyond the obvious advantages of the controlled access freeway, MacKaye saw such highways as barriers to suburban sprawl. With limited access, freeways could not produce the snakelike motor slum of service stations, hot dog stands, motels, and all the other small businesses that string themselves along principal roads where access is not controlled. In practice, this has been only partly correct. Freeways do indeed break up the motor slum, but the

* Reprinted as an appendix in the paperbound edition of his *The New Exploration, A Philosophy of Regional Planning* (University of Illinois Press, 1962).

placing of exits much closer together than I suspect MacKaye visualized them has spurred development of suburban "communities" in many essential ways not communities at all. We have understood only the lesser benefits of the concept and have missed the main advantage by not understanding the total idea.

This failure to understand MacKaye's proposals is doubly surprising because for the most part they are basic, straightforward, uncomplicated, so obviously filled with what we might call "Yankee common sense." This is especially true of such articles as "Region Building in River Valleys," published in the February 1940 issue of *Survey Graphic*. All that is required to arrive at MacKaye's conclusions is the ability to look at a region as an integrated entity rather than as a captive province meant only to serve its dominant megalopolis. The rest follows inevitably.

Habit and immediate profit are all that have continued our building of cities on river flood plains. We no longer need our factories right on the river for the flowing water to turn the waterwheel, nor does commerce and communication any longer depend primarily on the afternoon packet boat up (or down) from St. Louis. Our cities' water supplies do not depend on barrels filled at the bank of the stream. Yet we continue to crowd river flood plains with homes and stores and factories, and continue to be dismayed when the waters rise, as they do sooner or later. Then, of course, there will be a clamor for dams and levees and flood control reservoirs to protect values that have initially been created with no thought of flood dangers. Public money is sought to make good on bad private investments.

In his review of how the costs of such flood control projects are justified, MacKaye puts his finger on a primary difficulty in the evaluation of most such public engineering projects—how to weigh benefits that cannot be expressed in dollars and cents, how to value values. The planner or engineer who justifies his projects only in dollars and cents has missed MacKaye's point. The *quality* of the environment is the final test, and this requires the broad, qualitative viewpoint of the humanist rather than the narrowly materialistic view of what Benton's brother James called "practomaniacs" whose answer to every problem is the bulldozer and the concrete mixer.

If from his early professional interest in forestry, MacKaye's work has moved toward the community, whether town or city, and the works of man on flood control and transportation, it has at the same time moved in the opposite direction, toward the uses of the wilderness. He has been especially active in urging preservation of wilderness because the spread of urbanized civilization most immediately threatens this aspect of the balanced environment. MacKaye's concern for preserving wilderness has provided an excellent example of his ability to combine the visualizer with the practical doer. In the "Geography to Geotechnics" series he has described his origination of the Appalachian Trail idea and his role in the founding of the Wilderness Society, both of which have done much to preserve the opportunity for wilderness experience for the average American.

MacKaye considers wilderness a prime source for recreation. When he speaks of recreation, he means the word literally to stand for a re-creation, an opportunity for self-realization and growth by the individual. Like Thoreau, he does not "love" nature for itself, but rather he seeks to understand it as it relates to man. He sees wilderness experience as a way for man to return to the significant essentials, a place for the development of fuller awareness of the real meaning of harmony between man and the landscape. Man in society is always preparing a face to meet the faces that he meets. But in the wilderness man has the opportunity to encounter himself at last in elemental terms. It is in these terms that MacKaye can present the wilderness as a fit setting for meaningful recreation, and recreation, he reminds us, is the reason for industry.

Providing an opportunity for wilderness experience to the ordinary citizen is not just a holding action for Mac-Kaye. His plans are never static; the functioning of a viable culture is a dynamic process. Accordingly, his proposals for the preservation of wilderness areas represent the first step in a campaign that will use such areas as a base for an aggressive counterinvasion of the metropolitan sprawl, forcing wedges and slivers of wilderness and park land into the formless suburban mass to break it into manageable units that might then become coherent communities.

MacKaye deliberately overstates the case for his Barbarian, as he readily admits. His concept of the balanced man requires experience and understanding of all three possible environments: wilderness, rural, and urban. In an approach reminiscent of Crèvecoeur, MacKaye sees the man who knows only wilderness as a savage, lacking the development of his human possibilities through culture, the man who knows only the rural as a country bumpkin, trapped in the narrow considerations of crops and livestock, and the man who knows only the urban as the effete "civilizee" who has lost touch with the elemental sources and harmonies in nature from which we ultimately draw all that we are and all that we use. Unlike Crèvecoeur, however, he chooses the composite experience rather than the yeoman farmer as the mainstay of democracy.

For a stable culture, then, we need a balance of the three environments, and the true urban community is as much in need of preservation and even expansion as is the wilderness. The "barbarian invasion" of which Mac-Kaye writes is simply the first step in developing such a balance.

MacKaye's major concepts, and his own career, are effectively summarized in a series of seven articles published in 1950-52 under the general title, "Geography to Geotechnics." This series, which taken together constitutes an extended essay of almost book length, is second in length only to *The New Exploration* among his non-technical writings. In these essays, MacKaye traces the development of his own career as a geotechnist and the problems and progress of geotechnics in the United States. His insight into the interrelationships between the government of the new nation and the landscape that it governs is a fruitful approach to the interpretation of our political history. From the geotechnist's view, the settlement of America has been a process of the people's efforts to make the continent habitable. The problem lay in their lack of understanding of the principles of habitability and their tendency to think of their New World only in terms of their experience in the Old. The result was missed opportunities, waste, loss of habitability. Yet step by step, sometimes by accident, victories for habitability have been won. MacKaye outlines what these victories have been and plots a course for capitalizing on them in the future. The entire process comes down to a race to preserve habitability and establish the general practice of geotechnics before the environment has been finally and irretrievably destroyed. When civilization was only a few clearings on the eastern seaboard and the forest was being attacked only by the ax, ignorance of the principles of geotechnics seemed of little consequence. Now, with a population of hundreds of millions and with gigantic machinery cataclysmic in its effect on the land, such ignorance costs a higher price than we can continue to pay. As our reserve of unspoiled environment has dwindled, our speed of using it up has increased. We are wasting a decreasing resource at an increasing rate. In such terms, a Spenglerian death for our civilization rushes toward us at an accelerating rate and looms over us even now.

Still, MacKaye does not accept this end as inevitable. He holds out hope through geotechnics and tries to point the way toward the use of our past experience and our hard-won knowledge of habitability for the solution not only of our basic environmental problems, but also some of our most pressing political problems. The entire globe, MacKaye reminds us, is finally the environment that we must consider, and habitability is finally the common concern of all mankind. If the peoples of the earth can unite in working toward that one goal, starting with some commonly held "folkland," perhaps, MacKaye suggests, some of the geotechnic advances that helped to bind the United States together into a single nation can be duplicated on a global scale to bind a disorganized and warring world into a single community of men in harmony with each other, society, and the physical environment upon which their lives, and the quality of their lives, finally depend. This for MacKaye is the ultimate goal of geotechnics.

The essays in this volume demonstrate that Benton MacKaye is a humanist not alienated from modern scientific technology, a champion of democracy and individualism who makes use of social planning, social science, and conservation. As a writer he has offered a new synthesis of technical knowledge with human values. As a planner he has long sought ways to develop participatory democracy without forfeiting the advantages of large scale social and governmental action. An essential factor in such a combination is a sense of community interest that can only be developed by an informed and interested public, and so his work as planner and as writer flow together into the role of visualizer and teacher.

Although MacKaye's writings are known among specialists in forestry and regional planning, they have not achieved the broad recognition that he has sought and that they deserve. His central concepts of indigenous culture and viable community life have not been put into practice. It may be that we have begun to pay a terrible price for our failure to do so. Pollution of our air and water we have begun to recognize and, haltingly, to remedy. We possess the necessary technology and wealth to complete that job, and someday it may be done. But pollution of the moral and intellectual streams of our democratic culture will be much more difficult to correct, the processes more difficult to reverse once well started.

Through most of the twentieth century, Benton MacKaye has recorded our civilization's steady destruction of indigenous culture and warned us of the consequences. He has shown us how the spread of megalopolis and motor slum has destroyed our cities and towns, replacing them with a rootless, formless, sprawling mass of cancerous urban growth. He has patiently explained to us many times over how the destruction of indigenous culture brings the loss of any sense of community, and how communityless people feel they have no real stake and no real influence in the conduct of public affairs. This in turn has led to mass man in his ugliest forms, and this mass man has given rise to the social technician who owes his allegiance not to his neighbors and his neighborhood, not to his community because there is no community, but rather to a bureau chief in some distant capital, for whom the social technician's activities are primarily a source of statistics and records.

History has shown that democracy is impossible when the people feel they have no stake in the community and no real control of its destiny, yet we have continued to foster just such conditions in our communityless urban centers. The worst consequences of this destruction of genuine community among our people have been riots in our cities, and there are ominous predictions of more riots to come. The most encouraging consequences have been the few clear voices raised in favor of a return to participatory democracy. But the people behind these voices must first learn the lesson that Benton MacKaye has been trying to teach them for so long. Participatory democracy cannot spring full blown on a federal level in a nation of 200 million people spread across a continent and half an ocean. Participatory democracy is a democracy in which the social technician does not dictate to mass man on orders from above, but rather works with individual men within a community to attain community goals. This, of course, requires the existence of genuine communities and not formless sprawls of people daily hurrying from where they would rather not live to where they would rather not work and back again, or worse still, have no work to do.

What we all want, whether we articulate it in this particular way or not, is the opportunity to develop our own individual potentialities to the fullest. MacKaye shows us that we can best do this if we escape becoming mass men and instead live in functioning communities where every individual interacts with his neighbors and feels he has both a voice and a stake in community affairs. The quality of our lives is much affected by the quality of our environment. We need the help of experts in achieving the highest possible quality, but finally the best will grow only out of our own aspirations and abilities and out of our own local—indigenous—experience and requirements.

These are the lessons that MacKaye has been trying to teach us. For many years we have ignored or misunderstood them. We have already paid a high price for this oversight. Someday soon the price may bankrupt us as a culture, and the Spenglerian cycle will have again come full circle. Let us hope that instead we may still take the alternative path toward a stable and harmonious indigenous culture that MacKaye has tried to open before us. The hour is late, but the path has been marked.

part I

Geography
to Geotechnics

I

Growth
of a New Science

"The earth as a habitable globe."

William Morris Davis, 1898

"Your subject is geotechnics."

Patrick Geddes, 1923

Thereby hang two tales that merge into one, a story with a big question mark as to the ultimate success of mankind as inheritors of the earth.

These quotations, a quarter century apart, form the top guideposts of my own working career. Each was uttered by a master of his discipline—the one geography, the other geotechnics.

I shall always recall how Professor Davis began his opening lecture in "Geography A" at Harvard University in 1898. He gave it in the Agassiz Museum and he held in his hand a six-inch globe. "Gentlemen," said he (I quote from memory), "here is the subject of our study—this planet, its lands, waters, atmosphere, and life; the abode of plant, animal, and man—*the earth as a habitable globe.*"

Reprinted from *The Survey*, Vol. LXXXVI, No. 10 (Oct., 1950), pp. 439-42.

That was my guidepost No. 1, pointing me toward no mean field of work.

Nor, skipping a quarter century, shall I ever forget my first walk with Patrick Geddes (later Sir Patrick), the sandy-bearded Scot of Edinburgh, Dundee, Dunfermline, Dublin, Montpelier, Bombay, Indore, Jerusalem, Tel Aviv—with the whole epic of civilization visioned from his famed Outlook Tower at Edinburgh.

This was springtime in 1923 at the Hudson Guild Farm in the New Jersey Highlands. Geddes, "Jack of all trades and master of city planning," proved a fast walker for a sexagenarian though his tongue outdid his legs. But first he had asked me about my work and so had to listen as I recounted adventures in conservation under Gifford Pinchot and in regional planning (under nobody). I had delved back to geography under Professor Davis when Geddes rounded on me in the path.

"None of those!" he caught me up—"Not conservation, not planning, not even geography. *Your subject is geotechnics.*"

And then with a lunge he resumed speed, but only for a few strides. Again he stopped short.

"Geography," said he, "is descriptive science (*geo* earth, *graphy* describe); it tells what *is*. Geotechnics is applied science (*geo* earth, *technics* use); it shows what *ought to be*." And on he bounded.

"But what's the matter with 'conservation,' " I pleaded, "or 'regional planning?' "

"Nicknames," he retorted. "Of course you 'conserve,' and of course you 'plan' just as you do in building; but verbs like these stand for operation and make no term for your comprehensive science any more than 'nail-driving' is a substitute for 'architecture.' "

Once more he bounded on—while I trailed after him,

pondering his new word for my chosen field. He had raised my guidepost No. 2—giving me what I had searched for so long—its name.

Geotechnics! I wanted to use it right away, and like a precious nugget found in the path, I carried it hidden in the deepest pocket of my brain. I tried the term out on some members of our little "R.P." group, suggesting that "regional planning" was a makeshift only. In general they rose to it, but shared my own feeling that the time was not ripe. For one thing we had not seen it among the "geo's" in American dictionaries. Lewis Mumford, then a budding author, had sat at the feet of the Scotch master in his youth. It was he who had imported Geddes for us and he was quick to see both the virtues and the hazards in such a christening. I had similar reactions from Robert Bruère, Stuart Chase, Alexander Bing, Charles Whitaker, and Clarence Stein.

William Roger Greeley, Boston architect and planner, was also one of us, and one day I sprung the matter unexpectedly on him.

I gave him the word, *geotechnics,* and then asked him to give me his own idea of what it was all about. I was ready for his quaint and kindly humor which in this instance can best be conveyed in Mr. Dooley's dialect:

"About?" he says,

"It's about using the earth," he says,

"to make a living," he says,

"and," he says

"to enjoy the living when made."

"In other words," he says,

"to cultivate habitability."

Habitability! Here was the word to go with geotechnics —the precise yet comprehensive objective sought by the science to which Sir Patrick had given a name. That checked with "habitable globe," the term Professor Davis had used. So putting together Geddes and Davis and Greeley I had this connotation: "Geotechnics is the applied science of achieving for the habitable globe a greater habitability." Of course—if a bit clumsy.

Forthwith, in the 1920's, I proceeded to write about "habitability." Later, in the 1930's, when with the Tennessee Valley Authority, I gave birth to a long memorandum ("Opus One" they called it) on how to achieve greater habitability for that watershed. But never did I dare mention out loud the proper Geddesian term though I grew ever more impatient.

The 1940's came, twenty years after that prescient walk and talk with the late Sir Patrick. I was in St. Louis with the Rural Electrification Administration exploring how electricity could give farm lands greater habitability. I was about to use the real name anyhow, baptized or not, when, seated in the library, I found myself confronted by Webster's International Dictionary and turned to G. There I found it:

"Geotechnics—the applied science of making the earth more habitable." I swallowed a howl lest I should break the library edict of "silence." My inhibitions over the years evaporated. The name was now respectable. Once in the dictionary it could be employed in all companies— and with a definition better than my own. And so, at long last, the *name*.

Meanwhile, during those years and under various names, I had been working on the *thing*.

Clearly each name had expressed only some particular angle of that. Let us look at these names (and angles) as they have cropped out during the fifty years I have observed the growth of this new science.

Geography

The day's work has thrown me with a number of important geographers besides Professor Davis—men to whom every would-be geotechnist should be introduced. One was the long time geographer of the U. S. Forest Service, Fred Plumer, scientist and wit. Through him (in 1913) I met and had a long talk with Henry Gannett, then the illustrious geographer of the U. S. Geological Survey and president of the National Geographic Society—Gannett, whose opinion counted in checking the claimed discoveries of homecoming explorers, including Commodore Peary on return from his successful polar expedition in 1909. In due course, also, I came to know Isaiah Bowman, director of the American Geographical Society. On my desk as I write is a souvenir of an interesting hour spent with him in 1929—an article on "The Pioneer Fringe," itself a ground-breaking statement on the subject, published in the October, 1927 issue of *Foreign Affairs*. Listen to his first two sentences:

"We have reached the stage of a five-dimension world. To the three classical dimensions of space we now add a fourth dimension of *time* and a fifth, *quality*."

Bear in mind Bowman's "quality" whenever we use Greeley's "habitability." Indeed, more than anything else it is the *quality* that counts. Some land may be capable of supporting human beings only at a level that would not be worth living. Its quality would then be rated minus par; but the term "habitable," itself, as we use it, implies a quality equal to par or above.

This was my cue when, in the early Thirties, I had a job figuring on the habitable quality of the Tennessee River Valley for the TVA. . . .

There is another word stemming from geography which

should not be confused with geotechnics. This is geo-politics, which my dictionary defines as "the application of political and economic geography to the external political problems of states, notably problems of national power, frontiers, and possibilities of expansion."

Accordingly, geopolitics, as practiced by any particular "state," has the clearly implied objective of expanding that country's "national power" on the map of the world. Thus it becomes a polite term for geo-domination, a sort of game of force and intrigue with the globe as chess-board —in short, the super military strategy of aggression. Other countries are given the choice of surrender or devastation. The usual consequence, as evidenced in two world wars, is devastation—which makes the earth *less* habitable.

The end result of geopolitics, therefore, if not its theoretic objective, is diametrically opposed to the purpose of geotechnics—which is to make the earth *more* habitable.

Forestry

Forestry was still new in this country when I began to study it in 1903—five years after sitting at the feet of Professor Davis with his "habitable globe." Forestry may be defined as the practice of growing woods instead of mining them—one of the first great applications of science to make substantial portions of the earth "more habitable." Known for several centuries here and there in Europe, forestry was applied in America on a minute scale by William Penn and others in some early colonial ordinances of the seventeenth century. It remained, however, little more than a preachment in this country until well toward the close of the nineteenth century.

In 1891, the President was authorized by Congress to reserve from sale any forested portions of the public domain. Six years later, Congress opened these reserves for use and placed them in charge of the Interior Department; but it was not until 1905 that a study agency (U. S. Bureau of Forestry) became an action agency (U. S. Forest Service) and was authorized by Congress to manage our forest reserves.

These then comprised a domain of about the size of France; and their first manager was the late Gifford Pinchot—America's first forester, in time and renown. He headed federal forestry for twelve years—from 1898 to 1910—when he was unceremoniously thrown out of office by President William Howard Taft. Afterward, he was twice governor of Pennsylvania. In his own words: "I've been governor at odd moments but always I am a forester."

Along with Theodore Roosevelt, Pinchot had bucked the spoils system rampant in the public lands and their natural resources, above and below ground. While President Roosevelt was at the White House all went smoothly, but President Taft thereafter appointed Richard A. Ballinger, of Seattle, as Secretary of the Interior. Reversing Pinchot, Ballinger held with western ways; the public domain should be for private enterprise. To whom did it belong: (a) to an abstract collective people far away, or (b) to individuals and corporations on the spot? Theodore and Gifford had said (a); William and Richard said (b). Theirs was a dramatic, hard hitting bout by sincere men on the old issue of public vs. private use of natural wealth. In the long run, the principles of Roosevelt and Pinchot won out.

I had entered the U. S. Forest Service in 1905. That was its natal year, in the heyday of the Roosevelt-Pinchot regime. My first twelve months were spent in the woodlands and sawmills of New England, marking logs with lumberjacks and marking trees for country gentlemen. For some years I was in and out of the Service. While on leave I took a hand in organizing sundry landed institutions—the Harvard Forest at Petersham, Massachusetts; the Rhododendron Reservation at Fitzwilliam and the MacDowell Colony at Peterboro, both in New Hampshire.

Conservation

I was out of Washington during the big contest (Pinchot vs. Ballinger). From a distance this struck me as a fight for a folkland, to use the word employed by historian John Fiske. The land lay out west, in large tracts called National Forests. Together they formed a vast common heritage of the whole American people—hence a "folkland."

Now, each National "Forest" contained much more than trees. Along with timber went grazing land, or range on the mountain slopes. "Shoestring meadows," good for farming, bordered the streams below. Dotted along these streams were sites for waterpower. Coal and other minerals outcropped here and there. Wood, soil, power, ore, the "big four" resources, all were involved in one wide complex. Such was the Forest with a capital F. It belonged, in turn, to a complex of folks; it was National with a capital N.

Should it be Folkland or El Dorado?

Such, in essence, was the question that Gifford Pinchot put to the country. Could we mine coal and call it "forestry"? Could Uncle Sam as a forester prevent the stealing of waterpower sites? regulate grazing? and control a dozen other uses of the National Forest—in addition to selling timber? Yes, if not as forester then as custodian. The Forest Service was steward of the National Forests. The lawyers so held and the rangers so did (despite some local howls).

Name or no name the job was carried on. It was some-times called "land use" when I first became a forester, in 1905. Two years later (1907), the Forester, Pinchot, or his Associate Forester, Overton W. Price (maybe both), coined the term *conservation,* which is now part of the American language.

Meanwhile, the fight had centered on sources of power —water and coal. The most spectacular instance was that of coal lands in far away Alaska. The story of this made a drama that swept the country. In lieu of "Treasure Is-land" we had the then all but mythical Alaska; in lieu of "Captain Kidd" there was a Wall Street syndicate.

The coal seams remained in Uncle Sam's possession, but the uproar started public interest in the territory as nothing since the gold rush in the Nineties. How should it be developed anyhow—its coal and its other resources? Bills were introduced in Congress. Everybody had no-tions. I had one myself which was introduced in Congress by Senator Miles Poindexter, of Washington, in 1913. This projected a dual system for mining and selling by the government to provide a yardstick for coal prices. A bill (not Poindexter's) was finally passed which kept the lessees. Time was not yet ripe, however, for the yardstick.

That was to come twenty years later (1933), not in Alaska but in the Tennessee Valley, with water power rather than coal at stake.

Often linked with "conservation" is another term— "multiple use." The former applies to land; the latter especially to water, but both to the watershed. Closely associated with Pinchot's conception and development of the National Forests was his work with President Theo-dore Roosevelt's Inland Waterways Commission (1907). Thus Pinchot worked from both ends of the watershed: in the forests downward from the headwaters; on the waterways upward from the main stream. Hence, conservation and multiple use went hand in hand on American watersheds.

This big concept, according to Pinchot himself, sprang chiefly from Dr. W. J. McGee, head of the Bureau of American Ethnology. In *Breaking New Ground* (Harcourt, Brace & Co., 1947), Pinchot wrote: "McGee, at least as much as any one man, was responsible for formulating the plan for TR's Inland Waterways Commission, which for the first time considered the wise handling of all the natural resources of the continent as a single problem."

Thus was inaugurated, through the combined leadership and brains of Roosevelt, Pinchot, and McGee, the notion of the watershed as the unit of water-plus-land-use development. Its evolution occupied the bulk of "TR's" second term (1905-1909). A few years later (1911) the idea was applied in the Weeks law for the federal purchase of forest lands. Following this came the Newlands River Regulation Bill, the first legislative proposal for an over-all division of the continent into major watershed units. This never became law, but its long sponsorship by Senator Newlands of Nevada laid the basis in the public mind for the ultimate acceptance of watershed development in general and, in particular, under spur of Senator Norris of Nebraska, in the TVA.

Meanwhile, in prewar Washington an interesting group of young men was set going by my roommate, William Leavitt Stoddard, then on the *Boston Transcript*. We met regularly in "Stod's" office, a baker's dozen of us. There were three brands: (1) newspaper men, among them Stod and Fred Kerby and Charles Ervin; (2) government men, including Walt Durand, Hugh Hanna and myself; (3) institutions on two legs—Judson King, Lynn Haines, and Harry Slattery.

Engineering

Foresters themselves had come to be called "forest engineers," and members of the Society of American Foresters were put in *Who's Who in Engineering*. Later, it was apparently decided that foresters were beyond the pale and they were dropped from subsequent editions of that professional publication. My work, however, often brought me engaging teamplay with engineers.

One was Marshall O. Leighton, of the U. S. Geological Survey. Congress in 1911, in enacting the Weeks law, had authorized federal purchase of private forest lands at the headwaters of navigable streams—provided that forest cover really affected stream flow. Did it? The Geological Survey was designated to get the facts, and Leighton was put in charge. Under him an elaborate system of stream flowage measurements was set up on several watersheds in the White Mountains of New Hampshire.

The geologists, however, were not equipped to do the other half of the job, namely, to measure the amount of forest. So the Geological Survey borrowed a forester from the Forest Service. I was the forester and spent the autumn of 1912 in the watersheds, mapping the extent and density of their forest cover. When the two sets of measurements were put together they brought out the influence of forest cover on stream flow. So the area was acquired and became the White Mountains National Forest.

A generation later, on a similar study in New England following the great floods of 1938, I encountered Kenneth W. Ross of the Federal Power Commission. His main concern is rivers. Ross is what an engineer should be, a mixture of discoverer and inventor. Or we might call him a river psychiatrist. He can psychoanalyze the behavior of "Ol' Man River" better than anyone I know. He knows it is as natural for a river to flood as for a man to sneeze. Let's have, says Ross, "bigger and better floods," but so well controlled that every inundation shall, as in the land of Egypt and its Nile, spell fertility, not calamity.

Closely associated with Ross in the work on flood control were three men. One was William P. Dryer of the Federal Power Commission, an engineer who senses the power in a river as Ross senses its flow. The second man was Edward N. Munns, of the U. S. Forest Service, chief of the Division of Forest Influences, which reckons with the effects of vegetation cover on stream flow. The third was Bernard Frank, of this same division. Munns and Frank are also stream psychiatrists: they work on a river's upstream conduct as Ross works on its downstream antics. Bring these men together on upstream vs. downstream questions of river behavior and they would go far toward solving its complexes.

So much for geography, forestry, conservation, engineering—four of the names under whose auspices I have worked on the "thing" concerned with "making the earth more habitable." There are three more on the list before coming to the proper Geddesian name—*geotechnics*.

2

From Homesteads
to Valley Authorities

Colonization

As meant here, *colonization* was a new use for an old name. It had nothing to do with Old World "colonialism," which in these times is giving way in the Orient but was liquidated in the New World with the American Revolution and the subsequent sweep of wars for independence in Spanish America. Colonization was the name used by people in particular regions in which I once worked—the cut-over or "stump country" of the Great Lakes Basin and in western Washington State. I made a study of the subject as part of a joint project engaging the U. S. Forest Service and the U. S. Department of Labor (1915-1919). Mine was a study essentially of the relation of land and labor.

This bedrock relationship perhaps has never been stated more concisely than in the opening sentence of John Stuart Mill's great classic on Political Economy: "The factors of production are two, labor and appropriate natural objects."

Since natural resources form the basic "natural objects," the Forest Service was concerned with one factor, the De-

Reprinted from *The Survey*, Vol. LXXXVI, No. 11 (Nov., 1950), pp. 496-98.

partment of Labor with the other. Mill's thesis, indeed, has been rephrased in picturesque fashion by a forester, Raphael Zon, to whom *land* is the "mother" of production, *labor,* its "father." Zon himself holds the primary place in the *science* of American forestry that Gifford Pinchot holds in the American forestry *movement.* Incidentally, Zon happens to be my oldest colleague in the Forest Service, our friendship dating from 1905.

But we need neither Mill nor Zon to see that all workers must have "objects," or raw materials, on which to "labor." We recognize *land* in its widest sense (resources), as the ultimate source of the worker's livelihood. This massive fact was the driving force in the long fight for the passage of the Homestead Act finally signed by President Lincoln in 1862. That helped bridge the wide gap between the worker and his "natural objects." If a man lost his job or business in the East he might get a free farm out West. Even more, such claims afforded footholds of opportunity for young people. Thus was the West largely settled— but by 1915 free homesteads of any earthly use were getting scarce.

Now it happened that a "land man" held an important labor position. He was Louis F. Post, Assistant Secretary of Labor under President Woodrow Wilson. Post had been a close friend of Henry George and was himself described as "Single Taxer No. 2." The kingpin question with "Uncle Louis," as he was called, was this one of land and labor. How to make them meet? He proposed what amounted to a new homestead policy, trimming the old of its salient defects and developing what remained of the public domain under titles insuring "opportunity for profitable employment." In other words he sought to make the country more habitable for its inhabitants as *workers*.

The joint study was made, and I was the "hired man,"

working closely both with Post and Zon. The result was my report called "Employment and Natural Resources" (U. S. Department of Labor, Office of the Secretary, 1919). This covered all resources but centered chiefly on two—forests and farm lands.

First, how give the forest worker *permanent* employment as well as "profitable"?—how enable the roving homeless lumberjack to become a stable citizen?—how live in a community instead of a camp? This requires forest culture vs. forest mining; it demands cutting forest "interest" vs. cutting forest "capital," and doing it all within "commuting distance." I illustrated such possibilities in a plan for the Snoqualmie National Forest in the Cascade Mountains.

Second, how to enable the settler to make a farm out of stump land without becoming a speculator himself or the victim of one. Such a possibility had been demonstrated by land reforms working successfully in Australia and New Zealand.

Based on this study two bills were introduced in Congress and supported by the Department of Labor. One was the National Colonization Bill (H.R. 11329, 64th Congress, 1st Session, 1916), introduced by Representative Robert Crosser of Ohio; the other was the Public Construction Bill (H.R. 15672, 65th Congress, 2nd Session, 1919) by Representative M. Clyde Kelly of Pennsylvania. Hearings were held, with attendant publicity and education but neither was passed. The line of attack was never completed and may still be considered "unfinished business."

Regional Planning

It was early in the 1920's, a little before my walk and talk with Patrick Geddes, that I took up regional planning.

Though the sharpest shift in my career, it left me, as I have indicated, with the same goal—habitability.

The key problem from this angle of the subject was (and is) the movement and distribution of population (and indeed, ultimately, the size and locale of populations the world over). For me this was a new problem in "flowage." Heretofore I had grappled with the puzzle of *stream flowage* and flood control in examining watersheds. I had tackled the manner of *commodity flowage* (such as the marketing of wood products in the cut-over regions of the Great Lakes and Puget Sound). And now came this riddle which Geddes termed *folk flowage*.

What we might call the "headwaters" of folk flowage springs from big cities—out of which flows from every radiation highway an endless "motor slum." (That deft name is Walter Prichard Eaton's.) How to control this metropolitan backflow to preserve proper balance between urban, rural and primeval environments?

This last is a rock bottom question and I've taken my own fling in approaching it from each of the trio of environments.*

Being a forester, I instinctively began on the primeval environment. What should be major strategy in defending the primeval setting from the metropolitan invasion? This invasion was—and is—upsetting the healthful balance among primeval, rural, and urban influences. This upset is most rampant east of the Mississippi. Fortunately a wide mountainous underdeveloped belt, North and South, bisects populous states along the Appalachian Range. Here

* In Benton MacKaye, *The New Exploration, A Philosophy of Regional Planning* (Harcourt, Brace & Co., 1928). Paperbound edition with introduction by Lewis Mumford by University of Illinois Press, 1962.

lies the natural site for a primeval or primitive zone as a
major barrier to the backflows from big Atlantic seaports
and midland industrial centers. National Forests already
were established within this zone and if the public were
aroused National Parks would follow. But how focus the
public mind on a continuous wilderness belt from north
to south?

As a first step, my suggestion was "The Appalachian
Trail: A Project in Regional Planning" (put forward in
The Journal, A.I.A., October, 1921). This was conceived as a mountain wilderness path, for foot-travelers
only, throughout the length of the Appalachian Range.
My proposal was for local mountain clubs to work together
in making the Trail. This they did. In 1925, four years
later, the clubs federated in an "Appalachian Trail Conference," and during the following decade completed a
footpath spanning the more than 2,000 miles from Mt.
Katahdin in Maine to Mt. Oglethorpe* in Georgia.

The primeval environment—this, my first love, has
been an enduring concern. The Moses who was to lead
me *into* the wilderness was James Sturgis Pray, afterward
head of the Department of Landscape Architecture at
Harvard University. We met back in 1897, when the New
Hampshire White Mountains were almost all real wilderness. And now, half a century later, I find myself the hon-
orary head of the Wilderness Society.

The focus of our effort in this society is not a line but
a space—not a wilderness *trail* so much as a *wilderness
area*. This is the fresh minted name coined by a great nat-
uralist, the late Aldo Leopold. And a wilderness area is
just a chunk of wilderness on the face of the earth

* The southern terminus has since been shifted to Springer
Mountain.

(whether forest, swamp, desert, tundra, prairie, mountain, or ocean beach). But what is "wilderness"?

Negatively speaking, it is a place where there are no evidences of modern civilization—no traffic, no motor cars or boats, no sounds, signs or odors of man's mechanical activity.

Positively speaking, wilderness is what Thoreau called it—"the raw material of all our civilization." It is a natural society of plant and animal life dating back to the Silurian age, when life first left the ocean for the continents. From it our own civilization is but a recent offshoot. Howard Zahniser, executive secretary of the Wilderness Society, coined its significance in more homey terms: "Wilderness," he says, "is a piece of the long ago that we still have."

The Wilderness Society sprang from the imagination of a fighter for primeval America, the late Robert Marshall. It was this dynamic forester who, with the encouragement of a small group of which I was one (including Harold Anderson, Harvey Broome, Bernard Frank, Aldo Leopold, Ernest Oberholtzer, and Robert Sterling Yard) founded this society in 1935.

In my new guise as regional planner, I took a hand at the urban-rural problem. Since the turn of the century, our motor highway system has become the outer framework of civilization. The footway is essentially primitive; the motorway wholly artificial and, left to itself, begets motor slums.

The key cure for the motor slum is to promote a series of communities instead of one endless roadtown. This requires separation of functions; it demands the absolute divorce of *dwelling* from *through transport*—a problem which can be approached from either the town and dwelling angle, or from the road and transport angle.

Highways being region-makers, I chose the transport angle, and as major strategy championed "The Townless Highway" (*New Republic*, March 30, 1930). This avoids urban centers and bars roadside dwellings or other developments except at stations for entrance and exit. The Westchester County Parkways (N.Y.) were an early move in this direction.

Meanwhile, in 1928, two of our "R.P." band, Clarence S. Stein and Henry Wright, tackled the problem from the town and dwelling angle. They designed a "town for the motor age" which today is a structural demonstration of the principle just enunciated, namely the complete divorce of dwelling and transport. Through the creative leadership of Alexander M. Bing, this exhibit of a new framework for community life was financed and brought into being in northern New Jersey, under a name now known the world around—*Radburn*.

Economics

One more name I must mention in the list under which I worked at geotechnics:

In the Forties, the last three years of my governmental career brought me encounters with industrial economists no less than engineers. They were spent in St. Louis with the Rural Electrification Administration under my old friend, its then administrator, Harry Slattery. It was there that I dealt with *electricity* as a force for making America more habitable.

Incidentally I discovered some unlabeled geotechnists. One was the late M. M. Samuels, power engineer, author of *Power Unleashed*, philosopher as well as scientist.

The beloved "Sammy" of the REA, he was my boss at the start. My next was Franklin P. Wood, who with his assistant, John M. Duncan, made two more engineers whose philosophy consisted in replacing human sweat and muscle by kilowatts. But this labor saving campaign of the REA was combined with fiscal emancipation of the consumer. Kilowatts are delivered fairly "at cost" by co-operatives in lieu of the middleman's "price." My work in this phase of economic habitability brought me in contact with two masters in this field: one, Udo Rall, head of REA's Cooperative Education; the other, Paul Greer, rural editor of the *St. Louis Post-Dispatch*. Nothing rural or electric, cooperative, economic or geotechnic, escaped the attention of the unnamed lunch club that crystallized around this merry company.

Geotechnics

You have now the high points of my adventures in geography, forestry and conservation, in engineering, colonization, regional planning and economics. How to make these seven long words equal one (geotechnics)?

Genealogy may afford a clue, for ideas like folks are begotten one from another. It is indeed a fascinating process of reproduction which, in the span of five decades, I have had the good fortune to observe since my student days. In truth, the movement dates back to the colonial period, as we shall see in later installments. The era from Roosevelt to Roosevelt saw it take shape.

While Gifford Pinchot and his foresters in Theodore Roosevelt's time were projecting conservation, allied forces also were at work. Thus, Senator Newlands' River Regulation bill in Congress, with its "coordination of all the government agencies affecting water flowage," was one root of the concept of the "Valley Authority" which Senator George W. Norris carried to fruition in the Tennessee Valley. These and others were entering the general field of habitability through what might be called "Gate 1," or the *physical* approach.

Meanwhile, a root of quite another sort, namely, the coordination of the instruments of folk flowage, was growing up among the architects and city planners in Britain through such forerunners as Patrick Geddes and Ebenezer Howard, father of Garden Cities—and Raymond Unwin in the Greater London Plan of the 1930's. American contemporaries pushed out in the USA, entering the general field of habitability through what might be called "Gate 2," or the *social* approach.

Or put in old biblical style:

The foresters and their allies (Pinchot, McGee, Newlands, Norris, and company) begat—(1) conservation and multiple use.

The architects and their allies (Geddes, Howard, Unwin—yes, even our small R.P. band) begat—(2) regional planning.

Together, the two offspring begat—(3) geotechnics.

The work of this third generation took tangible form by Act of Congress in 1933—at the inception of the Tennessee Valley Authority. In the main this legislation was framed by the group concerned with conservation and multiple use. The contribution of the regional planning group was made in two short but significant paragraphs of that act.

Through Sections 22 and 23—savoring almost of a casual parenthesis—the concept of ultimate purpose in terms of the general welfare was injected into a code of detailed procedure as to handling flowage rights and surplus waterpower. The President of the USA, not the board of the TVA, was authorized, so far as Congress itself could authorize, to guide the "physical, economic, and social development" of the Tennessee River Valley for the benefit of "the people living in said river basin." The intent was to combine national viewpoint with local interest, while separating the process of long range design from the exigencies of day-to-day operative detail.

Those potent sections, 22 and 23, were written by two young planners, Frederick Gutheim and John Nolan, Jr. Later a member of the administrative staff drafted an Executive Order whereby the President signed away his own function as chief planner and placed it under the TVA board.

And so it came to pass that just as President Theodore Roosevelt in 1905 signed the bill which placed a vast domain of natural resources under conservation, so President Franklin D. Roosevelt in 1933 signed the bill which placed another such domain under geotechnics. This act of 1933 by no means spelled the last word in the yet crude science christened by Patrick Geddes. In 1950, we are as yet only at the threshold of any comprehensive effort at making our land "more habitable."

No more did the act of 1905 spell the first word in the conservation movement named by Pinchot. The public domain itself was born of the Ordinance of 1787 for governing the Northwest Territory in which Thomas Jefferson, drafter of our Declaration of Independence, had had a master hand. The first notion of major river development dates from 1785, with the inception of the Chesapeake and Ohio Canal. As we shall see later, this project of George Washington was not only to break ground for one of our first railroads, but as a waterway development, the C & O may be said to have begot the TVA.

In order then to get the story behind the story I have related, we must go back in my next installment to the birth of the nation and before.

3.

Genesis
and Jefferson

In my previous installment I defined geotechnics, scanned
its scope, and cited some first hand observations bearing
on its development in the present century. Now for its earlier American genesis, starting this off in biblical style but
fitting it to the pantheism of the American aborigines:

"In the beginning it was heaven on earth in the land of
America. There was but one environment—the primeval. And
the Great Spirit reigneth in the firmament where aery aircraft
snorteth not. And He had divided the waters from the waters,
those under the firmament from those above, in a perfect
hydrologic cycle. Floods there were in proper season on the
flood plains. These plains belongeth to the river; invaded not
were they by urban trespass. Verily, it was so. Dry land there
was which erodeth not, save at a rate only in eons told. This
indeed was good. . . .

"Grass gloried in mid-continent, and tree-yielding seed
spread forest east and west unto the distant shores. And the
waters did bring forth abundantly the moving creature that
hath life, not merely the fowl that flyeth above but moose
and bear and every beast that runneth or prowleth below.
Fruitful were they and multiplying, but in numbers not beyond the powers of herb and tree to yield a good standard
of living. Perfect to a microbe was the biologic balance. Believe it or not, it was so. . . .

Reprinted from *The Survey*, Vol. LXXXVI, No. 12 (Dec.,
1950), pp. 556-59.

"And man appeareth in this land of America, mayhap from the far Bering Strait. Red of skin and in feathered garb, he took dominion over fish and fowl and beast, but damaged not the sequence of their progeny. . . .

"And it came to pass that a new kind of man appeareth, of thin and bleached hide, but laden thick with gunnery. Suddenly, without warning, appeareth he on ships borne from far lands across the seas. By right of might claimeth he dominion over the land of America."

. . . And now in modern idiom listen to his story:

"The history of English settlement in America began on a beautiful April morning in 1607."—So say Nevins and Commager in the first sentence of their *History of the United States*. They go on to say that Captain John Smith was there and that his men were "almost ravished" to see such "goodly tall trees with such fresh waters." These seven words epitomize primeval America. The new Americans went to work on it—and with even less comprehension of their job than most of us Americans have of our job today. With vaguest notion of how to go about it they set out to make a continent habitable by the standards of their race.

From 1607 at Jamestown and 1620 at Plymouth, let us jump to 1776. By and large the original American scene was still nearly all intact. There were a few clearings in the solid eastern forest along the great interior path blazed by the French from Quebec to Detroit and on to New Orleans—via the St. Lawrence, the Great Lakes, and the Mississippi River. There were natural "oak openings" that antedated settlements to come in the hardwood forests of the Middle West—east of the prairies and the plains. But the main man-made openings were those of English settlements on the narrow threshold of the continent between the Atlantic and the Appalachians; also, in a couple of areas across the latter range on headwaters of the Ohio and Tennessee. On the whole, the primeval environment prevailed. The urban environment was limited to a few seaport towns, chief of which were Charleston, Philadelphia, New York, and Boston. Around these footholds a series of rural settings had been opened in the forest, making sites for thirteen little regional communities, each colony going its respective way of life under its own name.

Thus far had descendants of Captain John Smith's men (and others) rendered the continent habitable for the white men's needs. What next in the big job ahead?

To Make America More Habitable

Few of the modern problems of habitability were sensed in our colonial era. They were latent only, especially the riddles and paradoxes which were to arise with modern invention.

Take *social habitability*. Within each of the thirteen regions cleared for settlement the balance of environment was generally satisfactory. Much of the primeval setting was a liability to be pushed back out of the way. The modern invasion of urban influence upon the rural was undreamed of. Each town stayed put within its natural bounds. Boston was Boston and Cambridge was Cambridge; the agglomeration of a "Greater" Boston had not yet drowned civic sense in a score or more of once self-recognized communities.

The community *par excellence* was (and is) the colonial New England village. Take my own hill hamlet— Shirley Center, Massachusetts, as I knew it as a boy, with its seventy-one souls in the 1880's. A meeting house, a red brick schoolhouse, a store, farmhouses, wheelwright shop and town hall—seats respectively of religion, education, commerce, agriculture, industry, and government—

the basic elements of civilization. All were arranged around the "common" or "folkland," direct descendant of Anglo-Saxon commonweal.

Except for the motor car and plumbing, this description holds in large measure for Shirley Center today as I sit in my white clapboard house on one of its shaded streets and write these words. The New England community is yet a potent force which can play its part in our future and not a sweet old nostalgic myth to be fondly kissed goodbye. For one thing, it is the only community in this country, and perhaps in this world, where the town meeting functions as a true town legislature.

Problems of *physical habitability* were beginning to stir even in colonial times. However, they remained practically unrecognized. The notion of conservation was about as familiar to the average American pioneer as the binomial theorem to a Hottentot. Why otherwise? Here was the forest close at hand with its prodigious supply of fuel and housing materials. Here were the rivers to float corn to market, and their tributaries to turn the waterwheels to make the needed grist and lumber. These resources were appreciated as basic to building homesteads, but why worry about their future? Why think of replacing the forest when its limits seemed interminable? Just make another gash in the wilderness and move on.

Enter "Ecology"

In other words, our forefathers conceived not "ecology." We don't comprehend it yet, we ordinary folks. But it underlies the "how" of habitability: How to make the American or any other continent more habitable? So let us here and now add this essential term to our geotechnic vocabulary.

Ecology concerns the working of the "wilderness community." This I have identified in a previous installment as a plant and animal society, a wildlife civilization—whether swamp, desert, tundra, prairie, ocean beach, or forest.

Take the *forest civilization*. Take one of its several forest communities—the original white pine community of the northern Atlantic States. Who's who among its citizens? High in the social scale among the plant folk are the pine himself and his brother the hemlock, along with the shadbush, laurel and kindred undercover. Among the top animal folks we find the deer, the squirrel, "Brer Fox and Brer Rabbit," along with their feathered neighbors, the thrush and grouse. Lower down the scale we find lush ferns and mosses, along with their animal cousins, the turtles and the frogs. At bottom lie the "untouchables"—the worm, spider, and microbe busy mixing dead leaves with powdered granite to make the living pulsing humus that forms the community's floor and springboard. These citizens, high and low, left and right, work together, in competition and cooperation with the inanimate forces of nature, to create and carry on a perpetual and balanced way of life. "The how" of their working makes up the subject called *ecology*.

This concrete if complex picture can be seen on a woodland walk any day, but its significance is still vague in the popular mind. The term "community" applied to a forest, or other form of wilderness, savors yet of a figure of speech. So let us not blame too much our pioneer forebears for flouting its laws of life, for crashing into nature's delicate balances, for mining first the forest and then the soil, for setting up a "move-on" culture, ever seeking elsewhere a place in the sun instead of conserving a place at home.

Nature's Geotechnics and Man's Ecology

Ecology may be defined as nature's geotechnics; it is *her* "applied science" for "making the earth more habitable." She has made a great success of it. Back in the Silurian age, 350 million years ago, *land* was uninhabitable. So nature set out to make it habitable. First she made land a little habitable, starting on the Silurian seashores. Then she made it more habitable, in the lush growth of the giant fern forests of the carboniferous age. Thereafter—still more habitable in the wondrous vegetative landscape of this our present day.

Geotechnics may be defined as man's ecology. For it applies to human habitation; it is our *emulation of nature* in her successful effort to make the earth more habitable. To emulate nature we must study her. We must read directly in her open book. This our scientists have been doing in the centuries since Aristotle, and their tomes on the subject help fill our libraries.

Then plain folks, like the rest of us, read these tomes and thereby read nature second hand—or third hand or thirtieth. Most of us cannot read nature first hand; we walk or ride or sit in her midst and yet cannot grasp the story told out loud or spread out before us. When it comes to reading nature in the raw most of us are *illiterates*. . . . And unless we can do better than that collectively, we cannot truly emulate nature's art of living and survival—and thereby clinch our own.

Our chance to do this is close at hand. Nature spreads outdoor displays where we may see her working. Everywhere about us they occur in separate chapters. Chapter I unfolds the swamp civilization of horsetail, Spanish moss, and alligator (what the ecologists call the "hydrophytic" or wet community of wild life). There is Chapter II which visualizes the desert civilization of lichens, sagebrush and antelope (the "xerophytic" or dry community). Chapter III displays the medium or "mesophytic" way of wild life, such as the white pine community just described. There are further chapters exhibiting prairie, tundra, alpine, and other civilizations marking the pattern of primeval America.

It is these chapters that our New Wilderness Areas are designed to preserve. They are, if you please, open outdoor libraries wherein we can, if we will, shed our illiteracy and learn the lessons of the ages. And until we do this, not just "we"—a few scientists—but "we"—many citizens—our own human civilization cannot hold its place with any real security among other "civilizations," like those noted, which have fitted themselves for survival on this habitable globe.

And we have no time to lose. Go back to Bible times and read your Genesis and Exodus, with their accounts of folk flows shuttling back and forth between the lands of Canaan and Egypt in order to escape the famines resulting, then as now, from outraging "nature's geotechnics." And verily, man's *famine technic* the world over is keener now than ever as he allows the soil of his food-producing areas to slide into the sea while he creates his own image at a net increase of 50,000 head a day (William Vogt's estimate in *Road to Survival*). A poor geotechnist indeed is man, and we Americans have proven ourselves little better than the average since the days of our founding.

Jefferson as Geotechnist

Who among America's Revolutionary fathers stood out as geotechnists? There were several. Let me begin with Thomas Jefferson. He has been called "a land animal" as distinguished from "a salt-water man." Born and reared in inland Virginia, he turned his back on the ocean and looked landward. And in his looking he was perhaps the most nearsighted—and the most farsighted—among contemporary seers.

Jefferson's "Acadia" still lies deep in American folklore: the notion of a country of farmers each the sole sovereign of his *own* little hundred-acre domain. . . . "Those who labour in the earth are the chosen people of God" (1782) and "We have now lands enough to employ an infinite number of people in their cultivation" (1785).* But this astigmatism in his early forties he had shed by his seventies (1817):

"I was once a doubter whether the labour of the cultivator, aided by the creative powers of the earth, would not produce more value than that of the manufacturer, alone and unassisted by the dead subject on which he acted. . . . But the inventions of later times, by labour-saving machines, do as much now for the manufacturer as the earth for the cultivator."

Thus Jefferson lived to see the obvious need of a balanced over-all economy. Meanwhile his abnormal powers of "farsight" were making, not bucking, geotechnic history. To follow his farsight we must go back to the early 1780's.

With the fall of Yorktown (1781) a certain "people" in the land of America, to use his words in the Declaration of Independence, had successfully assumed "among the powers of the earth, the separate and equal station to which the laws of Nature and of Nature's God entitle

* *The Works of Thomas Jefferson* (in 12 volumes). G. P. Putnam's Sons, 1904, edited by Paul Leicester Ford who in the 1890's was editor of *The Charities Review* (New York), a precursor of *The Survey*.

them." Thus, alongside Britain and France and Spain, a new power rose in the New World. It occupied our Atlantic seaboard, but by the Treaty of Paris (1783) its flag was already perched on the far Mississippi. Thence westward to the Rocky Mountains "belonged" to Spain; and the land beyond—to any "power" with the power to attain it.

Even then, Jefferson's farsight reached from Monticello to the "Western Ocean." He had begun to think through two distinct plans for rendering more habitable the American continent. One was for the Northwest Territory, centering in the Great Lakes; the other applied to the farther "northwest" ranging to the Pacific. Perhaps he thought of the latter first. As early as December, 1783, he had written General George Rogers Clark: "How would you like to lead such a party?" Twenty years later, the general's son, William Clark, with Meriwether Lewis, under instructions from Jefferson, now President, *did* lead just such a party across the continent to Oregon.

Folkland vs. Colony

But Jefferson's plan for the "near" Northwest (present Middle West) was the first to be acted on. By the Treaty of Paris in 1783 the so-called "United States of America" came into possession (theoretically at least) of territory westward to the Mississippi River. The immediately important portion was the Northwest Territory—north of the Ohio River and bordering the Great Lakes. All colonial claims to this area by the separate (if "United") States had been virtually turned over to the federal government by 1784, making what John Fiske called the first American "folkland" (in his *The Critical Period of American History—1783-1789*).

What now to do with this great area held in common

by a people newly come among the "powers of the earth"? Should there be a big mother power on the Atlantic seaboard and a colony or colonies beyond the mountains? Or, should incipient states be established in the folkland later to reach equal standing with the original thirteen? Which scheme to take—the ancient institution of colonialism, or the new, untried experiment dubbed "statehood"? The answer at bottom was easy. With the late colonials, *colonialism* was well out of fashion. Jefferson's *statehood* plan, first projected by him in 1784, was adopted in essence at least by the Continental Congress in the Northwest Ordinance of 1787.

Two unique territorial institutions were established by this act—the statehood system and a public land system. But Jefferson's plans for the interior went further. He had in mind, also, a transportation system. He would connect the Ohio waters with those of the Atlantic by a series of trans-Appalachian canals. Like Washington, he feared disaffection otherwise, in the course of time, in the interior settlements. He was especially desirous of connecting the upper Ohio with the "Potowmac," and he took note of Washington's interest in such an enterprise. Thus he wrote to Madison from Annapolis (February 20, 1784):

"General Washington has (the navigation) of the Potowmac much at heart. The superintendence of it would be a noble amusement in his retirement and leave a monument to him as long as the waters should flow. I am of the opinion he would accept the direction."

Jefferson followed up his "opinion" by writing, on March 15, to Washington himself, suggesting that he take the lead in an Ohio-Potomac project. During his six months in the Continental Congress (December, 1783, to May, 1784) he wrote voluminously, especially to Madison, on problems of the "new" northwest. This portentous half-year was followed immediately by Jefferson's five years in France (1784 to 1789) as our emissary there. Perhaps it was during this period that he widened his global perspective and increased his "farsight." "More than any other American of his time," wrote historian Claude G. Bowers in *The Young Jefferson* (Houghton Mifflin Company, 1945), he "was conscious of America as a part of the world into which it had to fit itself."

America's Marco Polo

One way to this fitting, as Jefferson saw it, was via the Pacific as well as the Atlantic. Citing Bowers again, "As early as 1787, before the adoption of the American Constitution, he was dreaming of the day when there would be a Panama Canal linking the two oceans." He made inquiry concerning a rumored project by the Spanish government. This hemispheric concept seems to have sharpened his interest in the "far" northwest and in the expansion thither of a democratic nation. At any rate, while in France he resumed thinking in this direction—drawing on and giving encouragement to a new figure in American geotechnic leadership. This was an all but legendary hero of Dartmouth College—dubbed "America's Marco Polo" in *Passage to Glory, John Ledyard's America,* by Helen Augur (Doubleday & Company, 1946).

Ledyard was a Connecticut Yankee who as a young man helped to lay out Dartmouth College. He was the first and most elusive of Dartmouth's sons, and as a student hollowed out a big pine tree, the first white man to make the trip down the Connecticut River by canoe. Soon thereafter (1773) he joined no less than the explorer Captain Cook. For five years he sailed the seas, sighting America's Pacific northwest in 1778. Thereby he was seized of an ambition, traveled some more, met Jefferson in Paris

(1785), and set forth his ideas on economic global habitability and America's part therein.

Ledyard was one of the first to envision the world's sea lanes of commodity flow (furs and silks) and the strategic land link therein across the Rocky Mountains. So Ledyard, the "salt-water man" and Jefferson, "the land-animal," had come independently to ponder plans for the region of the "far" northwest. . . . The reader knows what followed—Jefferson's Louisiana Purchase from Napoleon (1803), and the Lewis and Clark Expedition (1806) bringing to earth Ledyard's dream.

Hence, Jefferson's "farsight," along with Washington's, covered the near northwest, and, along with Ledyard's, embraced the far northwest. Like these men, Jefferson designed as well as mapped; he was geotechnist as well as geographer. The essence of his design lay in the *folkland*. Not that this was his invention, for, in reality, it was centuries old; but he applied the conception to a continent. Not that he did this alone, but he sowed the seed in furrows that reached to the "Western Ocean."

The Secret of the Folkland

What, then, is the secret of the folkland (as against the colony) that was to distinguish the development of the USA? By what magic or hypnotism did a common stake in a remote wilderness cause new powers to keep their powers and yet set up a union above them?

Probably nobody has answered this question better than John Fiske. In analyzing at length the dangerous condition at the close of the Revolutionary War, he brought out how the thirteen supposedly "United" States—no longer united by a common fear, and not yet united by an effective common government—were fast becoming "Disunited" States. But as by-product of their independence

they had received from Great Britain a somewhat unex-
pected windfall—a common territory. Fiske then makes
his big point.

"Ever since the days," he says, "when our English forefathers dwelt in village communities in the forests, the idea
of a common land or folkland . . . had been perfectly
familiar to everybody."

Folkland consisted of "territory belonging to the
whole community," upon which new communities might
be organized just as they had been "in England before the
time of Alfred." (Witness the central "commons" sur-
viving to this day in *New* England, as mine and my neighbors' here in Shirley Center.) The 1780's in America saw
"the repetition of this process on a gigantic scale," namely
the creation of "a national territory beyond the Alleghenies
—an enormous folkland in which all the thirteen old States
had a common interest."

"Without studying this creation of a national domain,"
Fiske concludes, "we cannot understand how our Federal
Union came to be formed."

The conception of broadening this idea to include making the land more habitable appears to be Jefferson's own.
But in the good year 1787 (while Jefferson himself was
absent in France) it took the combined brainwork of his
colleagues in the Continental Congress in New York, and
of the colleagues in the Constitutional Convention in Philadelphia, to formulate, respectively, the Northwest Ordinance and the U. S. Constitution from which has come
that code of law whereby the land of America remains in
truth a folkland for her folk.

This folkland program speaks for itself as a grand and
good plan. Its far flung objectives and its rough hewn
machinery have forwarded the destiny of a nation dedicated to the pursuit of life, liberty, and happiness. In all

this—and in its vast endowment of education—the plan is *very, very* good. And in another sphere it is *fairly* good, namely in its saving clauses whereby to correct certain of its abominable defects. There are two of these, both of a geotechnic nature, which, together with their correctives, remain to be considered.

4.

Folkland
as Nation Maker

Along with its manifest excellencies, Jefferson's Northwest folkland plan contained the seeds of two baffling defects. One abomination was the layout of boundaries for the five incipient states. That was a simple, straight, and scientific system smacking of the surveyor's rod and glass but resulting, of all things, in a complex, crooked, unscientific hodgepodge. It may have been a necessary initial clay model but should have been brought to earth and corrected before it hardened.

This strait jacket for the new states, with a closer mesh of rectangular counties and townships, emanated obviously from the old British grants. Its deficiencies had been recognized even in colonial days.

Cockeyed Boundaries

"To settle the American governments," wrote Francis Barnard, Governor of Massachusetts Colony, in 1764, "it will be necessary to reduce the number of them, . . . and in general to divide by natural boundaries instead of imaginary lines."

Reprinted from *The Survey*, Vol. LXXXVII, No. 1 (Jan., 1951), pp. 14-16.

Compare this counsel with Jefferson's own conception: "I think," he wrote Madison from Annapolis in 1784, "the territory will be laid out by passing a meridian through the . . . mouth of the Gr. Kanhaway from the Ohio to L. Erie, and another through the rapids of Ohio from the same river to Michigan and crossing these by parallels of latitude 37° 39° 41° etc., allowing to each state an extent of 2° from north to south."

Thus each state was pocketed in a neat square, each with a Greek name lifted from Jefferson's classical education. The five states (Ohio, Indiana, Illinois, Michigan, Wisconsin) that actually came into being escaped the names and some of the boundaries.

But we cannot blame Jefferson. A wilderness is like an ocean—a blank on the face of the planet, a thing to be rendered comprehensible only in terms of latitude and longitude. Blame, if blame there be, must be placed on all concerned for not taking the sound advice of Governor Barnard as to "natural boundaries." This was everybody's business, and therefore nobody's. The result was a constellation of states which, though "regional," make poor "regions." Not one of them forms a rounded unit of development, or coincides with any natural or convenient scheme of flowage—of water, commodity, or population.

Here, then, was a marked defect in the original plan. The state, as devised in the Ordinance of 1787, was not a natural unit of growth or sovereignty.

The natural geotechnic unit of the early non-nomadic civilizations was the river valley, notably the land of Egypt, gift of the Nile. The natural boundary between valleys is the line along the ridge which separates their respective drainages (the divide). As a rough and ready rule, subject to very liberal modification, the basic seat of geotechnic development is the river basin or watershed, which is a cross-section of the land from top summit to ocean level.

This rule was recognized by international law in the days of exploration for new settlement. Invoking it, LaSalle in 1682, standing at the mouth of the Mississippi River, claimed for his liege, Louis XIV, the total Mississippi drainage basin from the Appalachians to the unknown Cordilleras. He called it the land of Louis, or Louisiana.

Let us improvise history. Suppose that on the "beautiful April morning in 1607" Captain John Smith with his lusty crew had *not* anchored near Chesapeake Bay, but at the mouth of the Father of Waters. Suppose their descendants, instead of moving "westward-ho" roughshod across range and river, had moved "northward-ho" up-river along the banks of Father Mississippi and his constituent children—the Ohio, the Missouri, the Tennessee, and his other tributaries. Suppose they had laid out state bounds on nature's lines instead of the cartographers'—on lines which separated one river valley from another instead of separating up-stream from down.

Such common sense cooperation with the law of gravitation, aside from its other benefits, would have saved a host of headaches for the federal courts, howls in the halls of Congress and barrels of ink in editorial offices. Every state would then have been just naturally a "Valley Authority" in itself. "State rights," so far as affected by stream flow, would be in harmony with the inexorable rights of Ol' Man River, and not be ever at outs with him—as badly as King Canute was purported to be with Ol' Man Neptune.

Between the institution of state and colony there is no comparison. As Jefferson sensed it, one is sovereignty and

the other subserviency. But pity 'tis that our state boundaries so seldom follow Ol' Dame Nature's. Nature's states
are the river basins; each is a sovereignty, one inside the
other—the Allegheny inside the Ohio and the Ohio inside
the Mississippi. Nature's states work together in perfect
harmony; their "compacts" have been worked out during the eons since the last geologic uplift of the land
mass. The closer man's states coincide with the Dame's,
the closer our regional sovereignty coincides with those
carved by our rivers, the better for us mere men. Jefferson's statehood scheme did not provide for this coinci-
dence.

The latest man-made instrument for so doing is the
Valley Authority. That ominous word "Authority" applies
to waters and not persons, and usually embraces parts of
several states. Persons go on about their business just as
they always have, from electing a Congressman to jailing
a town drunk. As a legal instrument, the Valley Authority
derives from the commerce clause of the U. S. Constitution. It is by no means perfect; it is still an experiment,
just as was the first steam locomotive. That implement was
based on the laws of pressure; this one, on the law of gravitation. The locomotive scared the horses and fell into the
ditch. The Authority may scare the politicians or dam the
wrong stream. In each case there are mistakes which are
subject to correction, but the principle is sound. The Authority is the outcome of a solid effort to bring man's concept (and practice) of sovereignty in harmony with nature
—and the river's.

Schools and Settlers

Having explored one shortcoming in the Northwest Ordinance of 1787—and before taking up another—let me
point out, parenthetically, that the founder of the Univer-

sity of Virginia was as much interested in the spread of
intelligence as in the trek of people to the Middle West;
that is, in equipment for citizenship that would go into the
building up to new states.

Once their cabins were up, settlers in those parts built
free schools. Thanks to Jefferson, there was history back
of that—for the Charter of the Northwest Territory provided for the greatest public endowment of education the
world had ever seen. In a region now the seat of five great
commonwealths, that charter set aside for school purposes
a share of every township. Through these land grants,
from crossroad schools to state universities, sprang the
public school system of the Great Lakes region which was
to set the pace for the whole West.

The Fee Simple Despot

Besides the statehood system, there was another major
feature of the Ordinance of 1787 affecting American
habitability. This was the public land system. Once the
United States came into possession of the Northwest Territory, it functioned in two ways—(1) as sovereign, and
(2) as land owner. In capacity (1) the USA divided its
sovereignty with future communities of the folkland; it
provided for their ultimate statehood. In capacity (2) the
USA divided its ownership with future citizens of the
folkland; it provided for their ultimate "landhood."

By this I mean something as definite for the single individual as statehood is for the community of individuals.
Statehood gives control (in part) to activity within a
bounded area of land. "Landhood" gives control (in
whole) to the land itself within a bounded area. This is
effected by "an invention of the Devil"—and of our re-
vered Anglo-Saxon ancestors. It is still worshipped at the
altar of Nordic tradition; its spelling is that of austere

Roman obeisance; it is the *fee simple* title to "real property."

Real indeed! It is real and absolute rule over a real piece of our real planet Earth. It amounts to private sovereignty over such piece. It is the alleged "right" of Farmer John Doe or of Lumberman Richard Roe to do whatever he pleases with his so-called "own." He may treat as he likes his own piece of earth with total disregard of everybody else. If he so desires, he may shove, or let it slide, into the sea—and he *does*. Messrs. Doe and Roe are doing this right now in (and to) the land of America. They are ruining, every year, as the result of needless erosion, half a million acres.*

"But," you say, "erosion is inevitable; every geologist will tell you that even mountains are worn down to level plains."

Surely they are. Nature herself is wearing down the face of the United States about one inch every thousand years. But in so doing she does not prick the skin of the earth's face. But man *does*. That is the whole difference between geologic erosion and man-made erosion. The "knife" man uses is of several brands—ax, plow, hoof, and fire are chief among them. Reckless logging, wrongly placed plowing, overgrazing, forest fires—by these methods man can do in a year what nature cannot repair in a century. But there are ways of preventing this bleeding process. They consist of proper methods of handling those "knives" (ax, plow, hoof, fire):

—Use the ax in the production forest, the kind best suited to growing timber, occupying generally the level ground or easier slopes; and chop no more each year than

* "Our American Land," Miscellaneous Publications No. 596, page 5 (U. S. Department of Agriculture, Soil Conservation Service), 1946.

grows. But spare the protection forest, the natural cover on the steeper slopes, which is chiefly valuable for checking rapid run-off.

—Plow along the contours so as to make terraces to check run-off, and not up and down the slopes to make gullies.

—Limit hoof to turf; limit the number of sheep and cattle to the capacity of the range—in short, do not overgraze it.

—Prevent forest fires.

All these things can be done and are being done. The ax is controlled in the National Forests and where timber cutting is conducted according to forestry. The plow is controlled on demonstration farms under cooperative agreements between farmers and the U. S. Government (Tennessee Valley Authority, or Soil Conservation Service). The hoof is controlled on the National Forests by grazing regulations. Forest fires can be fully controlled only by the great roving public, and only after it has gained some real sense of ecology. Meanwhile the various states, and the United States in the National Forests, are improving each year their fire prevention services.

One farmer to set an early example of plowing along the contours was the father of the public land system himself. Jefferson told what "we *can* do, if we care enough:

"We now plow horizontally following the curvature of the hills and hollows on dead level, however crooked the lines may be. Every furrow thus acts as a reservoir to receive and retain the waters; scarcely an ounce of soil is now carried away. . . . In point of beauty nothing can exceed that of our waving lines and rows winding along the face of our hills and valleys." (*Land Policy Review,* Bureau of Agricultural Economics, U. S. Department of

Agriculture, Vol. VII, No. 1, Spring 1944. Quoted on back cover page.)

Today, enough is being done to show what *can* be done to curb the country's bleeding sickness. But outside the meager proportions comprised within the National Forests and the other public reservations, national or state, the only way to check the aforesaid bleeding, under our free-for-all fee simple system, is for the *sovereign people* (of a state or of the United States) to go on hands and knees to each *sovereign person* (Farmer Doe or Lumberman Roe) and ask him, "Please, Mister, for our 150 million sakes as well as for your own one sake, treat in the right way, not the wrong way, your particular little chunk of our sweet land of liberty." Such after all is our present American geotechnic system.

Before leaving this subject, let me quote what the late Congressman William Kent of California, donor of the Muir Woods, said thirty years ago about fee simple before an annual meeting of the American Economic Association at Richmond, Virginia:

"In summing up, I arraign this traditional fee simple title for many economic and social crimes and misdemeanors. . . .

"It has contributed a great impulse . . . to the depletion of our agricultural areas; it has lessened our food supplies and increased their costs; . . .

"It has destroyed our forests, wasted our coal supplies, cascaded our petroleum.

"It has encouraged private monopoly and resultant extortion, and has encouraged malevolent activities by our common carriers.

"More than any other privilege it has permitted men to reap where they have not sown."

A Forest Folkland

As with statehood so with landhood, we are endeavoring to make repair. We are working to place some check on the private sovereignty bestowed by the Northwest Ordinance and the Constitution. And fortunately a check thereon was provided in the latter instrument. Turn to Article IV, Section 3, Clause 2:

The Congress shall have Power to dispose of and make all needful Rules and Regulations respecting the Territory or other Property belonging to the United States; . . .

If Congress may "dispose of" U. S. territory it may reverse the process and so reserve the territory; Congress may—if it will—hold any portion of the public domain from the clutches of fee simple. This, of course, only with land not already alienated. And Congress has so done. It has reserved *from* private sovereignty, and *for* public sovereignty, several kinds of special domains within the general one. Among these are Indian Reservations and National Parks. These have been created by separate acts of Congress. Finally, in 1891, a general policy of reservation was adopted and applied to the forest portions of the public domain, putting a check on the lumber sovereign.

This policy was contained in a short paragraph, Section 24, added to an act entitled "An Act to repeal timber culture laws, and for other purposes." One of the "other purposes" turned out to be the greatest timber culture law of all. Here it is:

Sec. 24. That the President of the United States may, from time to time, *set apart and reserve,* in any State or Territory having public lands bearing forests, any part of the public lands wholly or in part covered with timber or undergrowth, whether of commercial value or not, as public reservations, and the President shall, by public proclamation, declare the establishment of such reservations and the limits thereof.

This act was passed by Congress and signed by President Benjamin Harrison on March 3, 1891. Dr. Bernhard E. Fernow, who preceded Gifford Pinchot as head of the U. S. Bureau of Forestry, thus commented on the matter in his *Economics of Forestry*:

"It is upon this feeble 'rider' attached to a bill hardly germane to the subject that the forest reservation policy of the federal government is based, that the federal land policy, which before considered only disposal of the public domain, was changed, the government becoming a landowner for continuity."

President Theodore Roosevelt, guided by Gifford Pinchot's surveys of the forested public domain, did indeed so "set apart and reserve." Thereby came into being the bulk of the National Forests in our western country— a *forest folkland* the size of France wherein timber culture supplants timber mining.

We have now completed the first chapter of our genesis of geotechnics in the United States. We started (in my previous installment) with the primeval beginnings of the land of America; the advent of the white man and his settlement in thirteen separate communities in the Atlantic coast forest; his problems, latent and immediate, of making himself a home in a continental wilderness; his need of emulating nature's geotechnics in developing his own human ecology.

We have traced the part of Jefferson in this genesis, and his role as America's pioneer geotechnist; we followed his "farsight" across the continent, its focus sharpened by America's "Marco Polo." We cited his great plan for the region of the near Northwest, whereby the state, not the colony, became the unit of our expansion. We have noted certain flaws in this great plan, and with them remedies seemingly in character with Jeffersonian long-range principles.

We have scanned the geotechnic story of American land as such, and the role of the folkland as nation maker. Linked with this goes the story of American waters, and the role of their commerce, in turn, as nation maker.

5.

Washington
—and the Watershed

We have scanned what I called the first chapter of the genesis of geotechnics in America. Now for another and all but contemporary chapter. If Jefferson was the "Adam" of the first then Washington was forerunner of the second, for unwittingly he too was a geotechnist of sorts. The setting in his case was not a folkland but an inland waterway.

Before Washington was President of the USA he was president of the C & O—a company organized to put through a Chesapeake and Ohio canal, planned to connect the Ohio and Potomac Rivers with an extension to Chesapeake Bay. Through this project the father of his country was sire to its fortunes in altogether new ways.

As noted in my last installment, the United States of America started to become "Disunited States" right after the Revolution. One physically disunited section had become the home of settlers who had followed the trail which Daniel Boone had blazed across the Alleghenies in 1776. In less than a decade substantial populations occupied the upper waters of the Ohio and the Tennessee Rivers. Their outlet to market lay down the Mississippi as the Allegheny Range made a stout wall between them and the main body

Reprinted from *The Survey*, Vol. LXXXVII, No. 4 (April, 1951), pp. 172-75.

of seaboard citizens. These western groups began to feel neglected. Folks on the Tennessee actually started an independent state and called it "Franklin." All this looked bad to Jefferson—no less so to Washington, of whom John Fiske wrote in his *The Critical Period of American History, 1783-1789*:

From an early age he had indulged in prophetic dreams of the grandeur of the coming civilization in America, and had looked to the country beyond the mountains as the field in which the next generation was to find room for expansion. . . . In his early journeys in the wilderness he had given especial attention to the possibilities of water connection between the East and the West. . . . The subject was a favorite one with him, and he looked at it from both a commercial and a political point of view. . . . The East and West, he said, must be cemented together by interests in common; otherwise they will break asunder. Without commercial intercourse they will cease to understand each other, and will thus be ripe for disagreement.

Disagreements indeed! North *versus* South, East *versus* West. How to unite these regions? This was Washington's inveterate quest after Yorktown. He put it into words— including his famous "legacy" to the American people. His counsel as statesman was fortified by his bent as a civil engineer and his efforts as an unconscious "geotechnist." For his C & O plan to unite the East and West by fresh water—at right angles to the sea lanes, north and south along the coast—led early to the inception of a code of Union generally, and later to a *code of man* in harmony with the eternal *code of nature*.

Bull Session on the Potomac: 1785

In 1785, as president of his canal company, George Washington invited to his Mount Vernon home a few key people to talk things over—what we might dub a "bull session." This included James Madison, later President, and two state officials; one from Virginia, one from Maryland. They soon found they had bitten off a subject involving the whole question of commerce between the new states. Clearly this called for further discussion and wider representation.

Hence a second gathering the next year (1786) at Annapolis. All the new states were invited to send representatives. The purpose was to discuss commercial relations, not only along the Potomac, but generally. Alexander Hamilton stretched "commercial relations" to political relations and proposed another conference. That was held in Philadelphia. Those we now call the "founding fathers" met and spent the hot summer of 1787 in framing the Constitution of the United States.

Thus, step by step, from that little meeting of friends at Mount Vernon the "code of man" had its inception. But this is not all that emanated from it. There is another story and a much longer one, concerning critical portions of the Constitution's structure. It is the story of adapting man's sovereignty to nature's, of man's begrudging cooperation with river flow to make American watersheds more habitable. This story comprises the second "chapter" of our genesis of geotechnics in the United States—*on the role of American waters.*

Washington's C & O project was our first watershed enterprise in the first big scale use of American rivers: their use for navigation and transport. From the dawn of history the river had been the great highway for landlocked commerce. As such, on the new continent, it paid no heed to state lines if men chose to draw them in or across its natural lines of flow. That was man's headache— not river's. Washington recognized this when he asked officials from both Virginia and Maryland to attend his Mount Vernon meeting in 1785. The Potomac had been made a colonial and then a state boundary, thus requiring two sovereignties to deal with one river.

The framers of the United States Constitution cut this knot. They placed all interstate commerce, including river traffic, within one sovereignty (the federal) instead of among thirteen. Thus man's law was changed to conform to river's law *via* the crucial "commerce clause":

"The Congress shall have Power . . . to regulate Commerce with foreign Nations and among the several States, and with the Indian Tribes." (Art. 1, Sec. 8, Clause 3.)

High Decision on the Hudson: 1824

But in time that clause was challenged. Here's what happened. Back in 1798—when the federal government was cutting its first teeth—this commerce clause, along with the whole Constitution, was still a trembling experiment on paper. That year the sturdy New York legislature passed a sovereign act granting (for forty years) to Robert R. Livingston and the inventor, Robert Fulton, the right to "the exclusive navigation of all waters within the jurisdiction of the state . . . [by] boats moved by fire or steam." This grant in due time was assigned to another Livingston (John R.) who passed on to Aaron Ogden "the right to navigate the waters between Elizabethtown, New Jersey, and the City of New York."

Meanwhile, Thomas Gibbons was busily plying his own boats, in competition with Ogden, in these selfsame waters between the two states. Objecting to this competition, Ogden filed a bill in the New York State Court of Chancery, complaining of Gibbons and asking for an injunction to prevent his activities. Gibbons filed an answer, stating that his boats were operated under a license originating in the U. S. government by act of Congress of February 18,

1793. But Ogden got his injunction—and Gibbons appealed.

When the case finally reached the Supreme Court of the United States, the point at issue hung on the definition of the word—*"navigation."* Was it *"commerce"?* If so, Gibbons and the U. S. would be sustained (and the Hudson River along with them). If not, then Ogden, New York, and state rights would be the winners. Any school dictionary would seem to be the only document necessary to decide this early showdown between state and .federal authority. Nonetheless, the case, as recorded in 9 Wheat, 1, 6 L ed. 23 (U. S. 1824), ran to 100 pages.

Here was a definite call for "hands up"—a challenge to jurisprudence and economics (and to geotechnics). Would the feeble federal government dare to call the bluff of swaggering New York? The case was argued by an able federalist, Daniel Webster; the Chief Justice was John Marshall, early champion of the Constitution. It was not hard to show that navigation was commerce; everybody knew it. But these men were wary. Well must they have known that the whole fabric of union was being tested and that there was dynamite in any definition. So they were long in defining. Finally they came forth decisively with the obvious.

Marshall chimed in with Webster's claim as to the use of the word "commerce" in the Constitution.

Henceforth (Webster had argued) the commerce of the United States was to be a *unit;* and the system by which it was to exist and be governed must necessarily be complete, entire, and uniform. "Its character was to be described in the flag which waved over it, *E pluribus unum."*

The gist of Chief Justice Marshall's opinion:

All America understands, and has uniformly understood, the word "commerce" to comprehend navigation. . . . The power over commerce, including navigation, was one of the primary objects for which the people of America adopted their government. . . . The convention must have used the word in that sense, because all have understood it in that sense; and the attempt to restrict it comes too late.

The word used in the Constitution, then, comprehends . . . navigation within its meaning; and a power to regulate navigation is as expressly granted, as if that term had been added to the word "commerce."

Long afterward, Albert J. Beveridge, historian and senator, commented in his *Life of John Marshall*:

On March 2, 1824, Marshall delivered that opinion (Gibbons *vs.* Ogden) which has done more to knit the American people into an indivisible Nation than any other one force in our history, excepting only war. . . . [He] welded that people into a unit by the force of their mutual interests.

Ol' Man River as Uncle Sam

So Gibbons won. The Hudson won—and the American people. It was a triumph for sane jurisprudence and practical economics, and it was something more. It was a triumph for geotechnics.

The bottom winner of course—using the Mississippi's nickname, was Ol' Man River, dressed up as Uncle Sam. The laws of men bowed to "the laws of nature and of nature's God." A realm of man (a state) yielded to a realm of nature (a river). What was once sought for on the Potomac was realized on the Hudson. The "get together" at Mount Vernon had contemplated a single power over river commerce between two states (Virginia and Maryland). This power, as we have seen, was set forth in principle in the U. S. Constitution and its commerce clause. The power was now achieved in fact and law in the case carried to the Supreme Court over river commerce between two other states (New York and New Jersey). Americans deliberately revised their previous state line system to conform to the river's bland incomprehension of it; for state sovereignty they accepted river sovereignty, adapting themselves and their ideas to their environment.

But we have had more steps to take. Besides navigation, American rivers came to be put to other big scale uses— to irrigate land, to turn the wheels of industry, to light whole cities. These uses demand storage works whereby to hold the floods and ease their waters gently to the ditches and the turbines. So great dams and reservoirs have been built to catch the flow of water. They also catch the flow of silt. This raised another problem.

That silt must come from somewhere gradually penetrated the ivory-plated cranium of *homo "sapiens."* Why yes—from upstream and from the tributaries. After all, water flows downhill. But along with it flows good crop-producing soil to the tune of several hundred acres a day! I recall a ditty taught in the little red school house:

> Little drops of water, little grains of sand
> Make the mighty ocean and the pleasant land.

Brought up to date:

> Little drops of water take little grains of sand
> To the mighty ocean: result—unpleasant land.

There is no need, as we have seen, that this be so; most of the "little grains of sand" (and loam) can, with proper attention, be held at their upland sources. A previous installment of mine dealt with the U. S. Soil Conservation Service (SCS) and its demonstration farms which exhibit how this vast waste may be curbed by such means as contour plowing. Ax and hoof as well as plow can also be controlled. I told also of Engineer Kenneth W. Ross and his concept of "bigger and better floods"; meaning by that diversion of silt to low lands instead of sea, thereby spreading fertility along a river's course instead of havoc.

Indeed, we are only beginning to learn what can be done in allaying this bleeding sickness of the land.

For a great river is more than a river, it's a matrix of rivers like a leaf ending in a stem, or a bowl with a thousand sources draining to one mouth. Looked at this way, a river is part of a whole which consists of *water-oozing land*—its full name, river basin or *watershed*.

With water, as we have seen, flow silt and sand and soil of all varieties. Therefore a watershed is also a soilshed. This fact makes land use and water use all one thing. It makes upstream and downstream, tributary and stem—all one thing. It makes all parts of the shed, be they forest, range, or meadow—all one thing. The laws of nature which govern all these parts make up one law—which is older than any other sovereignty. It antedates the Silurian age; it is older than life upon the land; it is as old as water itself; it is *watershed sovereignty*.

The Rio Grande Decision: 1899

Recall, if you will, what was brought out earlier in this series about the crude layout of state boundaries, and hence of the states themselves, throughout our early American folkland. The distinction was drawn between natural boundaries and imaginary lines, between the crest-line (or divide between watersheds) and a parallel of latitude. Sometimes a state line followed a divide, but too often it followed a parallel or a meridian, or else ran through the middle of a river or diametrically across its flow. Then two or more man-made sovereignties were bound to overlap one nature-made sovereignty. By vesting over-all responsibility in the federal government, the U. S. Constitution sought to correct this confusion.

But the Hudson River case in 1824 applied only to the main stem of the stream. The navigation jam of Gibbons *vs.* Ogden occurred at its *mouth.* How about its *sources?* Did federal sovereignty include its tributaries as well as its stem? No case came up to test tributary river sovereignty in the Hudson Valley.

That was fought out three fourths of a century later, in 1899—and on the Rio Grande. The story begins with an act of Congress of September 19, 1890, which provided:

> That the creation of any obstruction, not affirmatively authorized by law, to the navigable capacity of any waters, in respect to which the United States has jurisdiction, is hereby prohibited.

Without authorization, a Rio Grande Dam and Irrigation Company made plans to dam an upper section of the river in New Mexico, and use the water for irrigation. On May 24, 1897, the United States moved in as keeper of river sovereignty. The Attorney General started proceedings to prevent the company from building the dam and appropriating the water. After various refusals to this demand in the lower courts, the case came before the Supreme Court of the United States, where Mr. Justice Brewer delivered the opinion:

> It is obvious that Congress (by the 1890 provision above cited) meant that thereafter no state should interfere with the navigability of a stream without the condition of a national assent. . . . It is not a prohibition of any obstruction to the navigation, but any obstruction to the navigable capacity; and anything, wherever done or however done, within the limits of the jurisdiction of the United States, which tends to destroy the navigable capacity of one of the navigable waters of the United States, is within the terms of the prohibition. . . .

"Navigability," not navigation!—that was now the point. The issue over *navigation* had been disposed of on the Hudson, back in 1824. Here on the Rio Grande was settled the question of *navigable capacity.* Moreover, tributaries were clearly and definitely brought into the picture of a flowing river. *Tributary sovereignty,* added to main stem sovereignty, enlarged the legal sphere of the river—and the watershed. Again Ol' Man River won.

Watershed Legislation

Twelve years after the Rio Grande case, Congress passed the Weeks Act (1911). Agitation for it had started around 1900. One purpose in mind was to save threatened wilderness areas in the "crowded East," and conserve a better balance between primeval and urban settings (social habitability is the geotechnic phrase). This idea was turned down by "Uncle Joe" Cannon, czar of the House of Representatives. He didn't "believe in buying scenery." The main object was forest production and the need of a continuous timber supply (economic habitability); but lawyers advised that neither crusty old Speaker Cannon nor the Constitution would allow government purchase on this score. Hence, those who favored the Act placed their reliance on navigation needs, which involved the control of headwater tributary streams; in short, watershed protection (physical habitability). This course panned out in the pioneer legislation of 1911. The Weeks Act provided that if studies showed that forest cover influenced stream flow (and hence navigability) then Uncle Sam, regardless of Uncle Joe, could buy the necessary cover (with the scenery thrown in).

I had a little hand in this process myself. The next year (1912) I was lent by the Forest Service to the U. S. Geological Survey to appraise the forest cover on the watersheds of the White Mountains in New Hampshire. This range (*via* the Weeks law) became a National Forest along with others throughout the Appalachians. Thereby, the National Forest System expanded from west to east;

thereby Congress recognized upstream watershed sovereignty.

I recall a little fun on that White Mountains survey. My boss was Raphael Zon, America's greatest technical forester. Coming to inspect, his time limited, he asked me for a bird's-eye-view. I took him to a point near Mt. Carrigain. He looked, noted, and without speaking, pondered the ecological panorama. Closing his notebook with a snap, he turned around:

"Mac, you've brought me to just the right strategical spot. I've got my dope. Now let's get out of here. Can I catch my train *tonight?*"

I snatched out my watch. "It's now twelve-thirty," I reported. "We have just five hours of daylight. It's fifteen miles to the end of the woods. Come, we can just make it!" We legged it back down the trail. Zon gulped and followed after, almost on a run. "Hi, not so fast, Mac!" "Yes, but we must." . . . Down the ridge we went and along the stream below. "Can we make it, Mac?" "Walk, don't talk." . . . We legged it through the Notch together and headed for Twin Mountain. "Can we make it?" "Shut up and *walk*." . . . Then 5:30, just light enough to grope our way. But we were out of the woods and on the big highway. Raphael Zon was panting but he'd been game—and he caught his train.

With the Weeks law enacted, the watershed was to come into its own. True, Congress considered, but did not enact, a wider application of watershed sovereignty. But in 1913 and after, Senator Francis G. Newlands of Nevada held the floor for his River Regulation bill. He divided the USA into its truly "basic states" (my name, not his), composed of the river basins. For each he set up his famous coordination of river-concerned agencies dealing with forest, soil, power, and stream flow.

During these years—the century's teens—contention waxed warm on the issue of public *vs.* private control of water power. Part of the wealth in flowing water lies in its latent energies. As Uncle Sam now controlled the water, he controlled its contents—whether "little grains of sand" or kilowatts. So he claimed and so Congress passed the Federal Water Power Act of 1920. The hero (or culprit) in this long waterpower fight was Senator George W. Norris of Nebraska. He kept at it, and won. Along with Weeks and Newlands, he lived to introduce, struggle for, and see signed in 1933 by President Franklin D. Roosevelt the most complete act to date invoking watershed sovereignty. As Pinchot was to the first Roosevelt and Norris to the second Roosevelt, so George H. Maxwell was to Senator Newlands, and Judson King to Senator Norris. Except for these men, Maxwell and King, we still might be waiting for the vision of the watershed to come to earth in the Tennessee Valley Authority.

The New River Decision: 1940

There were people who still held "There ain't no such animal!" and again they went to law. For, after all, after the Weeks law, after the Federal Water Power Act and, now, after the TVA, the courts had only in part recognized watershed sovereignty. The case of Gibbons *vs.* Ogden in 1824 had recognized public control of the main stream; the Rio Grande case in 1899, of the tributaries—but only as to "structures." Big dams were of course allowable, but how about this forest cover stuff (Weeks law)? . . . How about these iniquitous public waterpower rights (Federal Water Power Act)? . . . About all that rubbish as to watershed management in general (TVA)?

The answer came on December 16, 1940, when the Supreme Court gave its decision in the New River Case, U. S. *vs.* Appalachian Electric Power Co., 311 U. S. 377:

The power of the United States over its waters . . . arises from the commerce clause of the Constitution. . . . The federal government has domination over the water power inherent in a flowing stream. . . . In our view, it cannot properly be said that the constitutional power of the United States over its waters is limited to control for navigation. . . . Flood protection, *watershed development,* recovery of the cost of improvements through utilization of power, are likewise parts of commerce control. . . . That authority is as broad as the needs of commerce. [Italics mine.]

Management of river flowage by the federal government, not only to float boats downstream and place structures upstream but to manage "flood protection," manage "the water power inherent in a flowing stream" and project "watershed development"—thus, in America, our "supreme law of the land" was made part of the supreme law of flowing water. Thus Congress was freed to make the most of it.

John W. Scott, lawyer and former member of the Federal Power Commission, commented on the decision in the *George Washington Law Review* for April 1941:

This pronouncement of the court will serve as a constitutional beacon light in the field of conservation. Congress has heretofore recognized, and now the Supreme Court places its *imprimatur* upon the fundamental concept that the water resources of America—the totality of things inherent in and related to proper watershed development, long illusory—belong to, and may be realized and possessed by the people of America.

One year after this comprehensive decision came a strong "postscript" clinching watershed sovereignty. In the Denison Dam case, U. S. *vs.* Oklahoma, 313 U. S. 408 (1941), the U. S. Supreme Court held:

We have recently recognized that "flood protection, watershed development, recovery of the cost of improvements through the utilization of power are likewise parts of commerce control." And now we add: . . .

Flood control extends to the tributaries. . . . For just as control over the non-navigable parts of the river may be essential or desirable in the interests of the navigable portions, so may the key to flood control on a navigable stream be found in whole or in part in flood control on its tributaries.

To say that no one of these projects could be constitutionally authorized because its separate effect on floods in the Mississippi would be too conjectural would be to deny the actual or potential aggregate benefits of the integrated system as a whole.

In this opinion two definite rivets drive home what earlier decisions had implied: (1) "Tributaries" are spelled out; (2) The "integrated system" of the "whole" is placed above the "separate effect" on any part.

From C & O—To TVA

So much for my story of American waters which traces the evolution of river utilization in the effort to enhance the continent's habitability. We have observed this development, step by step, and river by river.

First, on the Potomac (1785): Washington's small meeting at Mount Vernon to consider his C & O canal project leads to a session at Annapolis, which leads to a session at Philadelphia, which framed a Federal Constitutional Convention which contained the key commerce clause.

On the Hudson (1824): The commerce clause is challenged; it wins; commerce is held to include "navigation"; federal river sovereignty is recognized.

On the Rio Grande (1899): Commerce held to embrace "navigability"; tributary sovereignty recognized.

On the New River (*1940*): Commerce includes "flood protection" and "watershed development."

In each test, stronger and stronger waxes Ol' Man River (clothed as Uncle Sam). At each step, closer and closer the evolving law of man adapts itself to the eternal law of nature. Meanwhile—*On the Tennessee River* (*1933*), watershed sovereignty had come into its first full-scale demonstration.

A blind child, holding a stem, fingers along the veins until he grasps the broad mat that makes the whole leaf. Even so have Americans come to envision the river—first the main stem, next the tributaries, and finally the whole watershed. From C & O, with its vision of the part—to TVA, with its comprehension of the whole.

6.

From Continent
to Globe

"Damn you, keep your eye on the ball!'

Such was the poignant advice administered to me with tongue and boot by an exuberant football coach in the gay and rugged Nineties. Via head and hind I have always remembered it. It applies to many things, indeed to all things leading to a goal. It applies not only to making the most of a new continent, from aboriginal beginnings to an American folkland; it applies to the goal of a habitable globe.

Poignantly if less ruggedly I bequeath that challenge to every geotechnist; to every citizen with active concern for the future. The time has come to look forward and in this our thought must shift from matters continental to those global.

Is there one secret, more profound than any other, for leading us toward this final goal of earthly habitability? If so, what is it? Who has it? Let us ask the greatest of all experts in the matter, namely Dame Nature, who, during the ages since the Silurian, has been steadily making the earth more habitable. From all indications, her answer is to follow heaven's first law—*order*.

Reprinted from *The Survey*, Vol. LXXXVII, No. 5 (May, 1951), pp. 215-18.

Ways to Global Order

Whither the ways?

We can perhaps get our bearings by noting first those leading toward disorder. Two ways—both highly lighted —lead straight as turnpikes toward the blackout of order on earth and good-will among men. They are today's big two terrestrial menaces:

A. *Starvation:* human stomachs multiply while crop acres decline.
B. *Decimation:* men have found the means to destroy themselves wholesale.

On the other hand, two other ways—one highly lighted, the other dimly so—lead by various routes, and round about, toward the bright hope of earth order. They stake out two definite lines of approach in attacking these menaces:

(a) *Frontal:* essentially political efforts toward some form of global sovereignty and peace.
(b) *Flank:* economic and cultural efforts toward global solvency and social unity springing from interests common to all.

Menace *A* is both cause and effect of menace *B,* and *vice-versa.* The frontal approach hits especially at menace *B;* the flank approach directly at menace *A,* indirectly at *B.*

Lest this "algebra" grate on the reader, let me draw on historical analogy. Take the situation in our incipient "United States" immediately following the Revolutionary War. There were two main menaces (which were already partly fact in the 1780's): economic depression caused by upset foreign trade; and internal dissension among the new States. Then as now there were two approaches to these menaces—frontal and flank. Both were tried by various leaders of that day.

Flank Approaches

Thus Washington first made a frontal appeal to the thirteen Confederated States to form themselves into a full fledged national government, issuing his famous "Legacy to the American people" (1783). Now Washington had the greatest prestige of any American then living; yet his political attack dragged.

Whether conscious or not of its full import at the start, he tried a second and economic approach—as brought out in my last installment. He had quietly set to work on a pioneer transportation project, the C & O Canal reaching through to western settlements in the hinterland beyond the Alleghenies. In this connection, his efforts at Mt. Vernon to compose conflicting sovereignties in the Potomac between representatives of Virginia and Maryland bore fruit two years later at the Constitutional Convention in Philadelphia. As we have seen, only less significant than the enduring framework for political union set up there under his chairmanship, was its crucial interstate commerce clause—establishing federal sovereignty over rivers as a means for trade and communication in knitting the new Republic together.

Returning to twentieth century history I take my cue from Washington's experience with frontal strategy. I am not writing on world government. I am concerned with geotechnics, with a series of activities aimed at starvation and decimation. The activities consist of flank attacks on these threats both to global order and human well-being.

Such efforts are central to the role of geotechnists in today's world. They concern everybody everywhere. At least three international institutions are now engaged in prosecuting them. These are—in the economic field, FAO (Food and Agricultural Organization of the United Nations); in the cultural field, UNESCO (United Nations

Educational, Scientific and Cultural Organization); in the ecological field, the PACC (Pan-American Conservation Congress).

Statesmen and mass movement make first page headlines in their frontal efforts to achieve some manner of political, *de jure* union for the world of the future. Specialized agencies like these make the back pages in their auxiliary efforts to weave a fabric of *de facto* union. Let me cite no less an authority than Sir John Boyd Orr, founder and former director general of the FAO ("Can Mankind Make Good?" in the FOOD number of *The Survey*, March, 1948):

"While the Assembly of the United Nations is holding governments together at the top level; the specialized agencies can begin to build a new world from the bottom upward."

Sir John went on to say that FAO food plans work at a level where "political and ideological differences are not so acute," and that "concrete collaboration of this sort lays foundations" for world government.

There are several ways, or routes, for this bottom-upward strategy. They traverse ground covered in the previous installments of this series from the angle of geotechnics, ground where "political and ideological differences" are least acute and where, therefore, humankind should find agreement most readily on *what we have in common*. Let me visualize these routes as running roughly parallel along a slope, those closest to nature at the bottom, those most affected by man along the top.

Terrestrial Consciousness

We start at the bottom level with a quotation from William Vogt in his *Road to Survival* (Wm. Sloane Associates, 1948):

All of them [the people of the globe] have one thing in common. The lot of each, from Australian sea captain to biochemist, is completely dependent on his or her global environment. . . . One common denominator controls their lives: the ratio between human population and the supply of natural resources.

"Global environment"—this "one thing in common"— the sense of it, what I call "terrestrial consciousness"— that, I submit, is the starting point of the way of ways to global order.

Environment is what's outside us; consciousness, what's inside. To get a *sense* of an environment means somehow to get inside us what's outside. This is easy when the environment consists of, say, an apple; once in the mouth we get a sense of it. But where the environment is a global one the feat is less readily accomplished—more akin, perhaps, to Jonah swallowing the whale.

But, fear not, just as the apple may be eaten a bite at a time, so the globe may be sensed one sense at a time. It's the fashion these days, for instance, to bite off the globe in the political sense, or in the military sense—and so on. What is now suggested is to try it out in terms of nature's works alone, untrammeled by politics, economics or any other man-made antics; in terms, that is, of *ecology*. Vogt, too, had this in mind:

Columbus, more than the atomic scientists, made ours one geographic world. Woodrow Wilson saw that we all live in one world in a political sense, and Wendell Willkie popularized the concept for the man in the street. However, few of our leaders have begun to understand that we live in the world in an ecological—an environmental—sense. Dust storms in Australia have an inescapable effect on the American people; they set mutton prices soaring.

Ecology then is short for the study of nature as a civilization in itself—that of the wilderness communities I have introduced to you. These go half way back to the beginnings of life on earth—which started as a biological colony along the shore of land otherwise devoid of plants or animals. From such shores hundreds of plant and animal communities have sprung. Each has evolved its own balance of life—a balance as delicate and complex as 350 million years might be expected to develop. Then man, with ax or plow or the hooves of his herds crashes into these age-old complexities and wonders why floods and dust bowls follow!

Crashing in on natural civilizations might be called an ecological crime. But it is one going on all over the world. That is why Vogt calls on us all to wake up and get an "ecological sense" of our global environment.

There are two distinct appeals involved. Vogt has referred to one—mutton prices. Besides this economic urge there is an equally definite cultural appeal. The two are distinguished in one of my local newspapers, the Fitchburg (Mass.) *Sentinel,* in an editorial stressing the need of wilderness areas.

"Our Common Bond"

One of the first basic observations on life in general, noted at least by boys, is the fact that two kinds only of men exist at whom no dog ever barks, but at whom he always wags his tail: (1) his master; and (2) the butcher man. The dog wags his tail at his master for sheer affection; he likes the butcher for that extra bone handed out to him.

Similarly, there are two compelling causes for man's liking the wilderness: (1) his affection for his first ancestral home; and (2) his survival interest in the source of ham and eggs.

Why, then, wilderness areas? Why save the primeval environment? In the world at large and right here in Massachusetts? (1) For the reason the dog loves his master—for what the primeval environment *is*—a common spiritual and mental bond, an endless interest to all men; and (2) for the reason the dog likes the butcher—for what the primeval environment *has,* for what the wilderness (if not "barked at," and lacerated, and eroded) is willing to hand out to us—a decent physical living, a "bone" for each and all of us, wherever we may be, and without the need of shoving and warring in order to get our share.

Here are twin appeals to soul and body. The pursuit of terrestrial consciousness, step by step, by a world people, constitutes what I should call the bottom road among the various flank routes leading toward global unity and order. It is this ground route which unfolds the nearest demonstration yet, not of peace on earth, but of a scheme wrought by ages since the Silurian, combining perfect control of life's eternal cycle with measured progress from lower to higher realms.

In sharp contrast with the ground route, we may visualize the top route, or political level. This deals only with the institutions of men, seeking order by man-made control of human action. The ground route we may call simon-pure *natural;* the top route simon-pure *artificial* in its best sense. Between them run others combining in varying degree the works of nature and of man.

We geotechnists must keep to the lower levels. I have just set up a guidepost to ecological common sense, so to speak, at the bottom level. Let us see how we can make a start to blaze its path.

William Vogt himself suggests a lead:

One of the most promising educational devices, which up to the present has scarcely been experimented with, is the national and state park. These should be used—and where they do not exist they should be created—both to foster an appreciation of nature and to enlarge the understanding of natural processes.

Here in all their fascinating complexity and interest can be seen the great plant climaxes, associations, competitions; the movements of the hydrologic cycle, the building of the soil by which we live, the environment and interactions of wildlife.

"To enlarge the understanding of natural processes."
These seven words mark out the bottom road to consciousness of a global order. Read nature in the open, first-
hand and not third-hand or thirtieth. Learn your ecology
from the ground up for it is nature's expert way, developed
through the eons, of making the earth more habitable.
Geotechnics, as I have said before, is man's ecology. So
we must have our *laboratories,* alias wilderness areas and
national parks; but we seek global—not just local—order,
so we need such laboratories the world around.

Nor do we lack movements in this direction. One such
is being led by the Pan-American Union—an effort,
launched a decade ago, which has taken form in a Wildlife Treaty, already signed by two thirds of the Pan-American countries, including the USA and Argentina. The
treaty offers a basic pattern for parks and preserves
throughout the two American continents to conserve flora
and fauna in their natural habitats—along with geological
formations and primitive conditions generally. A similar
plan was projected even earlier in Africa. Advancing these
ideas is a body with an interminable name: "The American Committee for International Wild Life Protection."
This committee expresses the hope that the American
and African movements

. . . should serve as a basis for discussions which will lead
to the establishment of a World Convention to further Nature
Protection through international cooperation. . . . Steps to
accomplish these results should be carried out within the
frame-work of the United Nations.

So we have people on at least three continents who have
developed enough terrestrial consciousness to sense the
notion of a *global wilderness;* not the kind to be wrought
by atom bombs but to be conserved around the globe,
parts of our original home of homes, for what *it is* and for
what *it has.*

Within the framework of the United Nations are a number of agencies representing flank or auxiliary approaches to the problem of global order. Take that quaint nickname UNESCO A project for global wildernesses to spread self-consciousness among the inhabitants of the globe would surely pass all three tests—educational, scientific, cultural. UNESCO, therefore, is at least one logical agency to explore and open up this ground route toward terrestrial consciousness and order.

Emulation of Nature

Having traversed a path on the simon-pure natural level, let us follow a higher contour with a mixture of natural and man-made elements. First, we must have a look at how this came about.

Homo, like *canis* and *felis,* is a predator (and, also, of course, a plant eater). Like wolves and panthers, presumably, he first hunted for his food; and when he lost his hairy hide he hunted also for clothing to keep him warm. For shelter, a cave or tree would do *pro tem.* Gradually he got enough skill to make himself a roof.

Then, slowly or suddenly, he did what no other brute had ever done before. He discovered the secret of chain reaction. He started a fire. Or lightning did it for him and burned up his primeval bailiwick. But in time he learned to stop as well as start a blaze, and use it meanwhile. Then and there a new economy was born.

This widened. Homo became farmer as well as hunter and found or made an opening in the forest. He learned the secret of seeds and became a semi-vegetarian. He tamed animals, milked, sheared, and slaughtered them. He had two worlds to live in—a rural world within the primeval.

Again his economy widened. He devised a wheel to

do his chores by placing it under a waterfall. With wheels to help him grind and saw, Homo became miller as well as farmer and hunter. Mills started towns. Hence, three worlds to live and work in: an urban world . . . within the rural . . . within the primeval.

Of these, the primeval is the product of all creation, and though often reduced today to scattered patches, continues ever potent if left undisturbed. Cities may come and cities may go but such a wilderness goes on forever. Its ecological civilization, its balanced vegetable and animal economy, maintain areas in perpetual habitability.

Can man, as geotechnist, do for the two worlds largely devised by himself (the rural and the urban) what nature has achieved in the uninvaded primeval? Unless he can, he must ultimately fail in preserving the earth as a habitable globe. In other words, we must match nature's ecology with geotechnics, or perish.

Is there some rule of thumb for this vast consummation? Verily, the first and simplest rule on earth: *Give back to earth that which we take from her.* Return the goods we have borrowed; in short, pay our ecological bills. Pay them in dirt, not dollars. It's the only currency the good earth accepts. Too long we have lived on dollar ecology. We've lived long because our principal in terms of natural resources has been huge. Today, the end is in sight unless we mend our ways. Not always can we dig food from rural field and spew it down urban sewer. Not without concerted replacements can we extract cellulose from rural woodland and grind it into urban newspapers. The ecological budget must be balanced or nought will remain to pay the undertaker.

Let me consult another seer—Fairfield Osborn (*Our Plundered Planet,* Little-Brown, Boston, 1948). "The order of nature," he writes, "can be expressed by the symbol of a circle" of which wild animal life was formerly an "inherent part." What has happened to that portion we have domesticated? To quote:

They [the domestic animals] end up in the consuming centers, their residues in disposal plants or carried to the ocean. The broader implications are that this holds true of a large proportion of the earth's products today, both animal life and plant life, including vast quantities of forest products. There is one steady movement of organic material to towns and great cities and industrial centers, there to be consumed or disposed of as waste but never to go back to the land of origin. We are hacking at the circle expressive of the organic unity and productive processes of nature. The question is: Will we one day actually break that circle?

Call it breaking the circle, or going broke, or squandering our ecological fortune, the only way to prevent vast depression and disaster is to balance outgo with income. Economics without ecology is a science in the air. In the two man-created realms—rural and urban—that balance is required for psychological reasons. The rural landscape demands protection from the urban slum. But also for low-down physical reasons, the rural well-springs (crop land, pasture, woodland) demand protection from urban leakage. Landscape is part of qualitative nature, or the thing she *is* to us; its treatment is a regional and local problem. Well-springs (or physical life sources) are part of quantitative nature, or the things she *has* for us. Their treatment is a continental and world problem. Of those parts of the world, subject to the spread of urbanization, Osborn writes:

The enormous and almost blind demands of the markets in great cities, sucking vast quantities and varieties of products from faraway land areas, may well be largely responsible for a process of land exhaustion that cannot continue indefinitely.

So much for the second route toward global order, the "emulation of nature." Having studied nature's geotechnics as applied to *her* special primeval economy, our aim is now to do as well by *our* own special economies. Of these, the rural comes first. On it the urban depends. Everybody knows that every city draws its sustenance from land (field, forest, or mine). Let us consider the renewable resources. Though renewable, are they renewed?

We take material from the field. Part of this (the protein) we use to maintain our human bodies; part (the carbohydrates) we use to pump our bodies with energy; part (the excrement) we sink in the ocean or dump into our rivers, there to poison the fish; part (the garbage) we largely dump in back lots, there to raise a stench and collect vermin. None of these materials, except here and there, do we put back in field and "circle."

We take material from the forest. Part of this goes into lumber, or paper, or other usable form, and is actually used. Part goes into slabs and part into sawdust piles. We are learning to salvage these waste portions, yet we are drawing from the (U. S.) forest "bank" about three times more than its income of growth.

No scheme to feed or improve the world can be financed on any but an ecological bank account; without this, gold is as worthless as paper; the only sound money is earth money. Osborn's circle of life (the ecological cycle) can be held together only by returning to it the *solid* substance taken from it.

The Cycle of Waters

Next we can follow the *hydrologic cycle,* maintained by *fluid* substance, the endless flow of H_2O from cloud to rain to stream to ocean to cloud. Water and life are so closely related that this cycle of waters is part and parcel of the total circle which binds our common lot on the heritable globe.

The watershed is the local theater of action, the river basin is a little water world unto itself. We have already scanned the watershed history of America, dating from 1789 when Americans began, under their new Constitution, to adapt human laws to the code of nature governing that portion of the cycle of waters flowing from summit to sea. We have seen how this new Constitution bowed to the cycle, and how on every legal test, from Gibbons *vs.* Ogden to the New River case, Ol' Man River, dressed up as Uncle Sam, came out consistent victor. The cockeyed geographic patterns of the various colonies did not fit the natural pattern of the watersheds; hence the state governments were excluded from jurisdiction and the U. S. government took charge.

Thus, in the United States, the legal problem of man vs. watershed has been basically solved—as dramatized in the valley authority set up for the Tennessee River. The TVA basin covers portions of seven states but with respect to the cycle of waters in this theater, one government controls, not seven. The TVA pattern is being considered for the Columbia and Missouri Basins.

What of similar watersheds on other continents? Progress has been made under the French on the Niger. What of the Ganges, the Yangtze, the Danube? Let us look at the last.

The Danube River watershed is larger than the Tennessee and like it overlaps portions of seven "states," Bulgaria, Rumania, Yugoslavia, Hungary, Czechoslovakia, Austria, Switzerland. These nations are theoretically 100 percent sovereign, but are often yanked about by real sovereignties wholly outside the basin.

But let's keep to the physical situation, for here is a geo-technic problem, like that of the Tennessee. But here man's law (or absence thereof) is still defying nature's law throughout the watershed. For the obvious good of its inhabitants it is patent that the flow of Ol' Man Danube should be managed as a single fluvial unit. "Fat chance," you say. . . . Supposing so, as would-be statesmen we must indulge in pessimism. . . . But as geotechnists there is nothing to prevent us from figuring out the physical problem. No, we cannot get all the data needed, but enough at least to make a thumb-nail sketch. I've done so myself, for the sheer fun of it, from data in a small atlas (plus a little hydrology that I happen to know). It beats crossword puzzles all hollow. . . . And if more people spent more time on real puzzles, and less time on blank ones, something real *might* come of it. Page the father of our country at his Mount Vernon estate.

I'm not sure which group of UN initials spells out the logical special agency to address itself to this problem. It would be one way to help the people of the world to feed themselves. Perhaps it would be another job for FAO, or for a "Point Four" project, or some other "bold new program." A start might be made by setting up a UN "Water Resources Policy Commission" based on the U. S. President's recent commission of this name, headed by Morris L. Cooke. In any case, it would be a flank attack toward global order, the self-same approach taken by Washington in seeking national order.

Perhaps what is needed on the Danube and on several other great split-up watersheds on this habitable globe is the precedent of some "supreme law" decisions—a Gibbons *vs.* Ogden, a Rio Grande case, a New River case. We have canvassed these decisions through which, under its new Constitution, the United States adjusted man's law to river's in all American watersheds. Similar legislation and decisions by a United Nations with similar authority would bring new life and resourcefulness to the world's great watersheds.

7.

Toward
Global Law

There is one field of activity which seems to bridge the gap between the essentially *physical job of land use* on the one hand and the *political job of law-making* on the other. Like a river, this is a movement or flowage from source to mouth; but it is a movement not of water but of commodity. It is a flow of food and fabric and fuel, of lumber and ore, from their sources in field and forest and mine to the mouths and backs and buildings of their ultimate consumers on town or city street.

Like the worldwide cycle of waters via stream, sea, and cloud, it is a world cycle of raw and finished goods via stream, sea, and land (now, also, through the clouds). This flow of things, like that of waters, has its gateways and bottlenecks and cockeyed artificial barriers; its high levels and low levels. It has the need, in common with all flowage, of some controlling hand, itself controlled or governed by the sentient folk affected.

Here perhaps is the most potent species of flowage, combining nature's ways with man's, the missing link between physics and politics. Its name is *commerce*.

It was this link between physical fact and political fab-

Reprinted from *The Survey,* Vol. LXXXVII, No. 6 (June, 1951), pp. 266-68, 285.

ric which the Supreme Court of the United States long since ferreted out in a string of decisions beginning with the Hudson in 1824. As we have seen, each decision was based on the commerce clause of the U. S. Constitution which in 1787 had proclaimed its original objective (freedom of commodity flow).

Thereby not only was the river itself freed from competing legal barriers but also the stuff borne on the river. Indeed, in these cases, it was the *stuff* that freed the rivers. A river big enough to be a natural highway of commerce must be kept navigable to carry it—by means of a steady flow from its sources throughout the watershed—state lines notwithstanding. The authority of the United States was made supreme over river flow—and over anything else affecting commerce flow. "That authority is as broad as the needs of commerce." (New River case, 1940.)

Recall the words of Daniel Webster in arguing the Hudson River case, 1824 (Gibbons *vs.* Ogden): "Henceforth the commerce of the United States was to be a *unit,*" a system "complete, entire, and uniform." Henceforth the continent's commodity flow was free to flow in all directions, on *land* as well as *water.* The movement of commodity and commerce in its essence is a world unto itself —a "unit" all its own. Like the river, it flows from source to mouth; like the full cycle of waters, it flows back from mouth to source. The essence of commerce is exchange. Imports must equal exports or the cycle runs down; and this in terms of stuff, not specie. "Old Jim" Hill, the railway king, put it in three words: "Carry no empties."

The Cycle of Commerce

We perceive, therefore, one great difference between the cycle of waters and the cycle of commerce. The first will make its round regardless of the acts of man; man may impede and divert this round to his own undoing, but he can no more stop it than he can stop the turn of the earth around its orbit. The cycle of waters is simon-pure physical. The cycle of commerce is physical plus political; it is a movement subject to nature's law and to man's law also. The latter may defy the former; and does so to man's sorrow. Any form of waste is part of this defiance. Man's special responsibility, then, in keeping the cycle going, is to *minimize the waste*.

There are two main forms of waste. One is material— the failure to return waste products back to the land to fertilize it (already considered by us). The other is functional—the failure to reduce waste motion (the subject now at hand). One is waste of *matter,* the other of *energy*.

The kind of commerce talked of in these pages is concerned with this latter waste. It is the commerce of commodity, not coin; of exchanging, not bargaining; it consists of the vast yet elementary process of charting stuff from countries having surpluses thereof to countries having deficits, and of keeping at it till we come out about even, carrying "no empties."

This is a far cry from modern orthodox economics. It is not the kind of economics that digs gold from the ground in one place so as to bury it in another; nor the kind that plows corn under so as to get more "bucks"; it is the kind aimed not to open up markets but to fill needs. It is economics of Sir John Orr's brand—in pioneering the Food and Agricultural Organization of the United Nations— namely, a "complete about-face" from the orthodox variety; it is the brand which would "provide food—not . . . to be sold, but . . . to be eaten"; the brand that we practiced in the late war when "we pooled not only production facilities and shipping, but raw materials and food";

it is the brand based on "the principle of common action" which led to the establishment of FAO. (See "Based on Human Needs," by Florence Reynolds, FOOD number of *Survey Graphic,* March, 1948.)

Commerce, roughly speaking, is only part of economics; viewed thus, it consists in distribution (transportation and the like) as distinct from production (farming, manufacturing, and so on). Commerce, too, is only part of geotechnics; as such it calls for charting commodity flow; calls for the realistic or physical approach of the FAO as against the artificial or financial approach of orthodox business.

Commerce as geotechnics can be boiled down and visualized on the map—as I learned to my satisfaction in attempting a sort of thumbnail chart of the world wheat crop. Using the best available statistics, on one little blue map of the world, I placed 100 *solid* circles, each in the center of a locality *producing* one per cent of the world wheat crop. On another map, I placed 100 *open* circles, each in the center of a locality *consuming* approximately one per cent. Then on a series of three maps I linked producing centers with consuming centers in ways which conceivably might cancel out the surpluses of wheat in some countries and fill the deficits in others.

At length all the producing circles were emptied and the consuming circles filled. There was no cross-hauling, no shipping of wheat from Podunk to Minneapolis and back again.

My plan applied to one commodity only—wheat. Of course, this grain would have to be paid for, and in terms of things, not money; real imports and real exports must finally balance. In any world planning, all main commodities would have to be comprehended, not in sign but in substance, before the Jim Hill doctrine of "no empties" could come to pass via minimum mileage (that is, minimum waste of labor and energy).

I recall a weekend at Hudson Guild Farm in New Jersey attended by a number of Europeans participating in the sessions in New York of the International Institute of Regional Planners. That was in 1925. We had a square dance on Saturday night and I can see now, in mind's eye, Sir Raymond Unwin, with coat off and vest on, prancing to the tones of the bull fiddle. On Sunday we all took a walk, and I can hear, in mind's ear, "Uncle Ebenezer" (Howard) roaring jocosely how to plan our little valley. . . . Our guests were not limited to British experts. The point of this story concerns two solemn Hollanders. I showed them my blueprints. They looked and pondered deeply, expressing their interest in newly acquired English. At length one asked: "How long this take you?"

"Oh, a few evenings last month."

"A month!" he cried, "mein Gott, I'd say a *year!*" Well, it might be worth a year, if only to enlist interest in this criss-cross puzzle of world trade.

In truth my little exercise was but a footnote to geotechnical research. While the statesman declaims in public hall, the geotechnist is out in the field or figuring in his den. Such seems to be the case today within special (auxiliary) agencies of the United Nations.

With respect to commerce we may ask: "Will the United Nations in our lifetime emulate the United States in Washington's?" We can point to Chief Justice Marshall's words: "The power over commerce was one of the primary objects for which the people of America adopted their government." Will some future "Marshall" some day say: "The power over commerce was one of the primary means by which the peoples of the world developed world government"?

At all events the cycle of commerce, no less than the cycle of waters and ecological balance on land, has a role to play in achieving order on earth. The charting of commerce offers one more flank route, whereby the geotechnist may complement the statesman in concerted efforts to make and maintain the earth as a habitable globe.

The World's Gateways

Taken in the abstract, such charting of commerce presents a fairly simple picture puzzle: how *in general* to feed the world—the word "feed" being stretched to include the filling of other human wants—whether soup, shirt, or shelter.

Imagine a huge square set up on an office wall, a school blackboard, or a barn door. Listed on its left are the natural resources (soils, forests, ores, fuels, power). Listed on its right are the human wants (food, clothing, structures, tools, energies).

Across the square we see the lines of commodity flowage—leading from natural resources to finished products like a great web. Take one line in the chart at a time. Take wheat, which flows from soil, to reaper, to grist mill, continuing in the form of flour to bakery and kitchen. Cotton flows from field via cotton gin and textile mill to garment center and clothing store. Wood (as logs) flows from forest to sawmill; thence onward as beams and boards to factory and lumber yard, and as pulp to papermill and the newspaper press room. Iron (as ore from mine) flows via blast furnace to steel mill and fabricating plant. . . . Meanwhile wooden chairs with steel nails turn up at furniture store and front porch. . . . Wholesalers and jobbers play their parts as way stations. And so forth—with a thousand other lines of flow that constitute the "blood system" known as industry.

Taken in the concrete, the puzzle becomes more puzzling: how to feed and clothe and house the world *on the map* of the world? Commodities flow, as in the chart, from natural resource to consumer. But every line of flow must have essentially a double track. Impossible! No, it can be done. Of course it *is* being done, else we would not be alive. Such is the modern problem of commodity flow, forth and back—boiled down to its raw, physical aspects.

Now add political aspects. Hamstring your lines of flow by man-made dams and tariff hurdles. Stretch artificial boundaries across the routes. These things we tolerate around the world like so many barbed-wire fences. They show up worst potentially at the world's bottlenecks, such as the famed big four—named Panama, Dardanelles, Suez, Singapore.

These great gateways for seaborne commodity flowage have interest innately common to all men. Yet they symbolize national vs. universal control—by the USA at Panama; by Turkey (partially) at the Dardanelles; by Britain at Suez and Singapore. Here are three sovereign "states," each assuming "among the powers of the earth" a "separate" but unequal "station." Each claims the right, within its "own" gateway, to regulate commerce originating or destined elsewhere.

Compare them with the new North American states under the Articles of Confederation and before the U. S. Constitution. As we have seen, Maryland claimed control of commerce on the Potomac River—the boundary between herself and Virginia. To George Washington, as a Federalist no less than a Virginian, this seemed a natural right belonging to the states as a whole. Failing to achieve his point by direct negotiation at Mt. Vernon in 1785, his efforts were successful at Philadelphia in 1787, when the framers of a Constitution for the new United States met under his chairmanship and wrote in the clause that gave to Congress the power "to regulate commerce among the several States."

Even so, New York in 1798 claimed the right to control commerce on the lower Hudson and granted a monopoly to and from New Jersey. A quarter century passed before the test came in the case of Gibbons *vs.* Ogden before the U. S. Supreme Court. Then, as we have seen, Chief Justice Marshall's decision in 1824 (with the Court behind him), placed control where it constitutionally belonged—not in Albany but in Washington.

So much for the Potomac and the Hudson, and after them the Rio Grande and the rest—under the U. S. Constitution with respect to commerce between the states.

Assume a United Nations Constitution with powers as real as those of the United States. Suppose this also embraced a commerce clause, giving to the UN power to regulate commerce among the several nations. Suppose an American named "Ogden" claimed rights in the Panama Canal under the U. S. Constitution; and that a Scotchman, "Gibbons," claimed equal rights under the UN Constitution. Then we would have another "Gibbons *vs.* Ogden" case—in name, in fact, in law. Would not once again a future "Marshall" be impelled to decide in favor of "Gibbons," and the broader sovereignty?

As with Panama, so with Suez and Singapore and the Dardanelles or any other bottlenecks which may attempt to harass or bar the free flow of trade. These gateways of the world should of course be world-controlled. I'm sure that Jefferson would have recognized this in his early vision of the Panama Canal. But such bottlenecks do not make the only squeeze plays. An invisible line of latitude across a river—if it is also a political boundary—may stop the flow, not of the river but of the commodities it carries.

All such man-made lines on land or water were blown away a century ago in the USA by the gust of our commerce clause. With similar winds around the world, global commerce, like American commerce, could become, in Daniel Webster's word, a "unit."

This is neither utopia, nor even free trade. Tolls might be collected here and there to cover construction costs and upkeep, such as those on sundry bridges and roads within the USA today. What this calls for is control of a common flow by the peoples who use it in common—a "supreme law of the globe" with respect to one thing, commerce.

Such law would go far toward rendering the earth more economically habitable. It will take time to develop. Meanwhile, as my thumbnail sketch went to show, visualization of the flow of commerce as a global unit is good strategy. Washington did its like in words when he said, "Let us bind these people to us by a chain that can never be broken." His reference was to settlers on the other side of the Alleghenies. What he said applies today to people on the other side of the world. The first "chain" he visualized as a harbinger of unity was the ditch of his C & O Canal.

Here, then, is one more flank route toward global order and law, the visualization of the commerce cycle.

Antarctica—Global Domain?

To keep down to earth: How about man's common stake in the land? In an earlier installment ("Genesis and Jefferson") we explored the potent influence springing from a domain held in common which was to become the seat of five great states.

We had the benefit of appraisal by John Fiske of the significance of the Northwest Territory, this common land or "folkland," made up of the fag ends of claims reaching

west, some of them to the Pacific and belonging to the
more fortunate seaboard colonies. These words from
Fiske's *The Critical Period of American History* bear
repetition: "Without studying this creation of a national
domain we cannot understand how our Federal Union
came to be formed."

Is there any such domain left in our day in any part of
the earth? Now, Mr. Geotechnist, keep your eye on the
globe. Clearly, the only substantial unoccupied land area
that you will find is the continent of Antarctica. That is
nearly as large as all North America; it contains natural
resources of great abundance and some say "fabulous"
value. True, unlike our Northwest Territory, it has no
latent fields of corn but it has untapped lodes of minerals.
These could make the base for profitable employment if
the Arctic continent proved capable of supporting life and
labor. The habitability to start with is surely not inviting,
but means for improving it may add an exciting question
mark to this age of surprise.

Antarctica, if not a homeland, might prove a mighty
storehouse. In any case it is being sought after. It is circular
in form, resembling a pie gnawed by icy oceans at the
edges. Already its map has been cut into several trian-
gular pieces, each having its apex at the South Pole and
its base subtending a segment of the outer border. These
pieces of continental pie are claimed by four separate,
sovereign, independent states.

As with Antarctica today, so with our Northwest Territory yesteryears. It was claimed by four separate colonies, turned states. Virginia claimed the whole of it; Massachusetts and Connecticut claimed parallel strips across
the southern portion; New York, the southeastern Iro-
quois country.

At first, these four American states were adamant

against giving up their respective slices. Gradually they calmed down and finally gained, literally, enough common sense to place their shares in the common pot of the new "United States." Thus was born the U. S. public domain, a common American folkland to the west. Thereby, as Fiske brings out, with their common stake in the Northwest Territory, the American states to the north, south, and east just had to unite.

How adamant, in turn, may become the several national claimants to Antarctica has not yet come to the surface. But if they should follow the American precedent, and place their shares in the common pot of the new "United Nations," Antarctica might play some such role on today's international stage as the Northwest Territory did in its day.

Thereby would be born a public domain of the United Nations, a common global treasure trove if not a folkland. By such an act the Fiske doctrine might be confirmed—a masterstroke toward order and unity for the whole world —from the bottom of the globe up.

This development at this stage is more political than geotechnical and I shall not pursue it further. It occupies the twilight zone between high affairs of state and low-down physical development. But let us leave it to the UN trusteeship system, one of several steps in the right direction by the UN, along with a "Point Four" program under the UN—rather than under U. S. or other auspices.

We have come to the end of our story. We have made the journey from geography to geotechnics—in my own case from the vision of William Morris Davis of a habitable globe to the dynamic concept of Patrick Geddes as to how to make it more habitable. . . . We have been observing the unfolding of an applied science—from the forester on one side, architect and engineer on the other.

Meanwhile, we have followed the genesis of geotechnics from its Silurian beginnings by Dame Nature—and from American initiatives by Jefferson and Washington, through to their more recent crystallization in the years spanning Roosevelt to Roosevelt. And we've taken a global look ahead.

No more than salient features have been noted of the scenes through which we have passed. Some of these have been stressed more than their due as life and labor goes on our planet. Normal ways of living naturally emphasize local and individual aspects, or those making for human and social habitability, what Thoreau would call the "quality of the day." . . . But the present juncture requires emphasis on wider aspects: on planet vs. region, on quantitative habitability vs. qualitative, on measures to meet what Alexander Hamilton would call the "exigencies" of "particular situations."

Our subject is geotechnics—how to use the earth, from dooryard to globe. In the normal years of yesterday we might stress the dooryard, but please, Messrs. Geotechnist, Statesman, Citizens all, in the urgent hours of our day— *keep your eye on the globe.*

The Gist of Geotechnics

Geotechnics concerns habitability. It is defined as "the applied science of making the earth more habitable." There are three kinds of habitability—I, physical, II, economic, and III, social. These are concerned, essentially, with three kinds of flow: Water (and attendant soil); Commerce (raw and finished materials and energy); Population (and attendant development).

I. *Physical habitability* is that quality of an area whereby its natural resources remain intact. To preserve this quality requires sustained use: soil fertility renewed; forest cut limited to growth; water tables maintained; restoration to nature of what is taken from her (including garbage and sewage), in a word—maintenance of ecological balance. . . . The key problems are river regulation and erosion control. The "region," or unit of activity, is the sphere of water flow, or watershed. *Synonyms:* conservation (of land and forest); multiple use (of waters).

II. *Economic habitability* is that quality of an area, or sphere of activity, whereby men and women are enabled to make a living. This involves the problems of commodity flow from natural resources to consumers, and the balance between surpluses and deficiencies. (From this angle: follow the commerce chart and "carry no empties.") . . . The "region," or unit sphere of activity is subject to two forces: (a) the centripetal, or flow from periphery to center, illustrated by the "milkshed" of a city; (b) the centrifugal, or flow from center out, illustrated by an electric power system.

III. *Social habitability* is that quality of an area whereby men and women are enabled to enjoy living. This involves movement of population, or folk flow. The typical "region," or unit sphere of activity, consists of a flow of people to and from a given metropolitan center and its environs. . . . The problem is to preserve a healthful balance between three essential settings or environments—the urban, the rural, and the primeval. . . . Factors playing creatively on these settings are the new community, the townless highway, the wilderness area.

Applied geotechnics combines all three kinds of habitability. The job is to make the earth, or any region thereof, all-around habitable. . . . Take TVA—a project which combines flood control, power development, and new communities—or put another way, the physical, economic, and social elements in making the watershed more habitable. The watershed is the geotechnic unit; it is something more than territory; it is a sphere of sovereignty, one pertaining to a river, namely, in this case the Tennessee watershed. That is part of a wider sphere of sovereignty, the Mississippi watershed.

Each sphere has its legitimate and equal interest: one local, the other over-all. Unfortunately, there is likely to be a twilight zone between them wherein their interests conflict. The job is to narrow this zone to the minimum. Indeed, almost every geotechnical problem (physical, economic, social) boils down to balancing sovereign interests between inner and outer spheres. In this, nature herself sets us some good examples.

In a word, geotechnics consists of emulating nature. Nature has a geotechnics of her own; we call it ecology; it consists of ways developed through the ages for making the earth more habitable. That is why ecology is nature's geotechnics—and geotechnics, man's ecology.

part II

Control
of the Landscape

8.

The First Soldier Colony
—Kapuskasing, Canada

While we in "The States" have been talking much (and doing nothing) about "land for soldiers," the little Kapuskasing colony up in Canada has been quietly at work in an endeavor to discover what there is in all our theories. The colony is run by the Provincial Government of Ontario. It has been in business for over two years, and some sixty families are actually settled "on the land." The writer spent last Christmas there and several days among the people.

This first soldier colony in America could be reached from New York by "blimp line" in a little shorter time than Chicago. You would steer northwest-by-north and land in the Canadian wilderness about half way between Lake Huron and Hudson Bay, just where the Kapuskasing River takes a big fall.

Kapuskasing is in the much discussed "Clay Belt" of northern, or "New," Ontario, on the National Transcontinental Railway. The whole Belt, flat as a somewhat wrinkled pancake, is covered by the forest of pointed firs that reaches one way to Labrador and the other to Alaska.

Reprinted from *The Public,* Vol. XXII, No. 1122 (Nov. 15, 1919), pp. 1066-68.

Crisp, dry air, which at twenty degrees below zero makes one "feel like a king"—such is the winter climate.

The westbound "National" stops every other evening at the little station and water tank. You pick your way gingerly back across the railway bridge over the roaring falls, to the east side of the river; then turn south along the wooden sidewalk toward the lighted windows of the central village. Next morning you see what this village consists of. There are neat frame houses, nineteen in a row, with one more called the "administration building," a big stable, a little clanging blacksmith shop, a planing mill, a warehouse at the end of the spur track, a handsome little school house, and (once again) a water tank high over all. These together constitute the community center.

It was about two and a half years ago that the Ontario Government decided to undertake the "soldier settlement scheme." The plan was to start a soldier colony on the timbered Crown lands of the Clay Belt. Each returned soldier in this colony was to receive the free title to a lot of one hundred acres, of which ten acres were to be cleared at Government expense (both "slashed" and "stumped"), with the understanding that ten acres more should be cleared within five years at the expense of the settler. The Government was also to build, free of charge, a house on each lot. The site at Kapuskasing was chosen and the project was begun.

There were last winter sixty-two settlers (with families) established on their lots. One of them, Mr. B——, was interviewed by the writer. He was a Cockney who had been all over the Empire. Father, mother, and six of the children were at home.

B—— came to Kapuskasing with the first installment of thirty-two settlers on July 5, 1917. He and his companions first lived in tents. He first worked at stumping and

building for the Government. The following April he selected his lot, the Government built his house, and in May
the family moved in.

B—— was in a position to know what had happened
"so far" in the colony. Things had by no means always
gone on "greased wheels," and he summed up the situation in this fashion:

"You see, the Government promised things it couldn't
keep to, but you should make hallowances and not hex-
pect them to do hall they claimed they would. But Hi
don't say that to them. Hi say to *them*, 'You promised
this,—why don't you do it?'

"The main place they've fell down is not gettin' stuff
'ere on time.

"Then there's poor organization sometimes. They 'ad
three men to a buzz-saw. One was a loafer and another a
talkin' fish. These men 'eld up the work of many others.
But we got them shifted round and then we did a lot of
work.

"Hi tells the officials what Hi hexpects of them, but
don't knock the scheme to the neighbors. In the long run
it'll work out hall right and Hi'm satisfied."

Other settlers mentioned other difficulties. Most of them
were "grievances" that could be remedied. But there were
some fundamental problems which as yet had not been
heard from.

All agree—enthusiasts, experts, and doubters—that
the Clay Belt, when "opened up" and "dried out," should,
in spite of the rigorous climate, become an excellent livestock country. They agree also that the soil is fertile and
capable of growing the hardier crops.

But the soil is "fertile" today precisely as New York
harbor was "navigable" in the days of Hendrik Hudson.
Associated with each are pitfalls. An accurate coast sur-

vey is needed in the harbor to locate the sand bars and the points of rock that wreck the unwary mariner. So in the Clay Belt. An accurate soil survey is needed to locate the *muskegs*—those "saucers" of sterile soil that wreck the unwary settler. The muskegs, like the sand bars, should be charted.

This is the object of so-called "land classification"— to chart the productive and the unproductive soils. And Canada, through her achievements in New Brunswick, is setting the pace in the development of this vital class of work. The lesson of New Brunswick, however, is not being applied at Kapuskasing.

Then there is the matter of locating and laying out the colony—the problem of "town planning." And a very *practical* question here is that of the dreaded forest fires. In the brush fires of 1916 whole villages in northern Ontario were wiped out and hundreds of persons perished. The country should be opened up in circular clearings, not in "tunnels" along the railroad.

Town planning is a coming line of engineering, and in this Canada excels. The adviser in this matter to the Dominion Government is Mr. Thomas Adams. He has developed systems specially adapted to the opening up of the community settlement and of Canada's wild lands, and his work is being taken up from one end of the country to the other. But not at Kapuskasing.

In the keen endeavor to let each man have what he wants, he is told to go out and choose his own lot. The result is that a large portion of the lots are sprawled out for eight miles continuously along the railway. This form of individualism, though popular at first with each settler by himself, is already unpopular with many of the people who now begin to see what is happening. The wives and daughters especially have become alive to the difficulty of getting together in a social way, and they seem thus to have scented sooner than the men a "grievance" that is basic rather than superficial.

"There isn't chances enough to have any dances," said a daughter of nineteen.

"Without we can get together," said a wife of twenty-seven, "to a card party, or a lecture, or something else— we might as well be dead."

But there is a third problem which almost none of them see—neither settlers nor officials. This is the question of land titles. Each settler will ultimately get his lot —one hundred acres—in *unrestricted fee simple*. The same old mistake of the homestead laws! The Dominion Government allowed the corroding homestead system to break up its domain of Crown lands in the Prairie Provinces just as our own government did with the public lands in our Prairie States. And now, when Canada wants land for her soldiers, she finds it has been "homesteaded" out of use. So she is suggesting expropriation to get it back again. This is well. But the time to "expropriate" is *before, not after*. This is the method in Australia. Not so at Kapuskasing.

The Kapuskasing colony, then, demonstrates some interesting points:

(1)   The "frontier" is not "isolation"—not, that is, if the community has anything approaching real organization. And without this, a farm anywhere may mean isolation.

(2)   Community organization (both for economic and social needs) means *self*-organization. Let there be plenty of "state aid" in getting started, but no paternalistic babying.

(3)   The colony idea gives utmost promise of success. So far it is actually working at Kapuskasing to the

benefit of the colonists. But there are three vital things that are not provided for—a thorough-going system of land classification, town planning, and a land tenure based squarely upon use. So long as these are lacking, the Kapuskasing colony, or any other colony, is doomed to ultimate failure in providing for the happiness of its members.

Kapuskasing shows big possibilities—so big that the defects shine out. The Ontario Government is doing pioneer work, in a social as well as a physical sense. Ontario and Canada generally have arrived at the "mistake stage" in constructive land development. Our own country has not yet arrived at this stage. The United States is making no mistakes about such development for the simple reason that she is doing nothing about it. In Canada they are making mistakes because they are attempting something. They are, therefore, to be congratulated. When shall we get started to catch up with them?

9.

End or Peak
of Civilization?

In place of a world, there is a *city,* a *point,* in which the
whole life of broad regions is collecting while the rest
dries up. . . . This is a very great stride toward the inorganic, toward the end.

Oswald Spengler

The end of what? Herr Spengler says "western civilization." If so then the big city (the metropolis) assumes a
dignity which calls for more than emergent plans to keep
streets open or to make more subways; it calls for a look
beyond the horizons seen from the top of the metropolitan skyscraper. So let us ascend the "Empire State" and
consider civilization.

Spengler says that civilization is a cycle like the four
seasons: it blooms in the spring, grows in the summer,
fades in the autumn and "dries up" toward the wintry
end. As it dries it concentrates—in "a city, a point." The
metropolis therefore is the harbinger of death. As the ancient Mediterranean civilization desiccated in Carthage
and in Rome so its modern counterpart is drying up in
Hamburg and New York.

Reprinted from *The Survey,* Vol. LXVIII, No. 13 (Oct. 1,
1932), pp. 441-44.

Henry Adams suggests that our civilization is a "comet." It consists of one big turning, not a series. Modern western society lives in the elbow of a parabolic curve following the law of the inverse square. Human society during the ninety thousand years preceding 1600 A. D. made about so much progress in mind and mechanism. During the three hundred years following 1600 A. D. it made an equal progress. Three hundred is the square root of ninety thousand. Adams (in 1909) queries whether this progression might continue (17 being the square root of 300, and 4 of 17). And would the curve straighten out again? Might there be a progression of 300, 17, 4, and then a straightening to 4, 17, 300, etc.? If so then the first half of the twentieth century would mark the turn of the comet of progress—the peak or culmination of development.

For development *in terms of the machine* this might well be so. And if so here is promise. The terrifying typhoon of the turning spell cannot last much longer, and parabolic peace must settle soon on a lengthening period of mental assimilation in terms of actual enlightenment. Mind yet may master ingenuity!

These two themes, put together, make an intriguing interpretation of the metropolis as the index of mechanical civilization. Spengler's theme suggests the end, Adams's the peak, of this civilization. Which is right? The answer transcends the wisdom of Solomon, Congress and the American press. We must wait a century or so and see. Yet we must live meanwhile—and act. But on what basis? Let us accept both themes, first one and then the other, and through them get a look at what is going on in the big world to be seen from the Empire State Building.

But first of all we shall define for present purposes the

little word "civilization" and at the same time we will try to briefly visualize its essence.

Civilization as a Flow

Physical outward civilization may be likened to a cobweb. At present a badly disheveled cobweb! It is a tangled network—a wilderness of metal threads (steel rails, copper wires, the routes of iron steamships) spread around the earth and woven here and there in compact knots (metropolises). These threads get entangled in various ways —mechanically, financially, humanly. Why shouldn't they? They reach around the world and are governed by a hundred thousand masters. When they get too much snarled they give forth maladies—congestion, strikes, hard times.

But outward civilization is more than just a maze. For the threads are hollow and serve as veins through which flows the blood itself—the vital *liquid* element. There is the flow of the world's goods (food, clothing, "things"). There is the flow of the folks themselves: back and forth across the map, and in migration to take up new abodes. the *essence* of civilization is a *flow*.

Let us look at both kinds—the flow of goods and the flow of folk: we shall consider them respectively with the two themes of history—of Oswald Spengler and of Henry Adams.

The Flow of Goods

First we shall accept Spengler's theme of history. The metropolis, "a city, a point," marks the end of the present western mechanical regime. The base of this regime is industry—not only western but world-wide, the fabric in which occurs the flow of the world's goods. Can this go on poorly functioning, or (as our historian suggests) must it rupture and finally disintegrate? Here is a problem indeed. Let us, from the top of the Empire State Building and via the airplane of the imagination, take cosmic flight in search of the perspective to see this problem whole.

We head outward toward the moon and then look back. What a meager object planet earth becomes—a little round cheese with yeast working here and there in small blotches that we dub "America," "Europe," "China"! The yeast appears to rise and fall in alternate war-like spasms and depressions. We go far enough away to get a truly cosmic view; then come in closer to study the surface in detail.

We find the "cobweb" of Earthian industrial civilization, a matrix of tiny streams—a veritable blood system —whereby the Earthians somehow make a living. Each stream is an article of need. We pick out three of them— silk, flour, nails—elements respectively of clothing, food, shelter. We follow their paths around the planet:

In China a stream of silk starts in a field, passes through a silk mill in Shanghai, flows in little drops called "spools" into a ship in the harbor, proceeds across the Pacific to San Francisco, and thence in streamlets to the housewives of America.

In America to pay the silk bill another stream arises. This starts as wheat on a North Dakota ranch, passes through a mill in Minneapolis and emerges on the other side as flour; as such it flows via rail to New York harbor, and via steamship across the Atlantic to Liverpool; thence in streamlets to the dinner tables of England.

In England the relay is continued. Two streams arise, one in Yorkshire of grains of iron ore—the other in Cornwall of lumps of coal; both streams flow via rail and meet at the smelters in Birmingham where they coalesce and form a single stream of pig iron. This passes through a nearby rolling mill, emerges as a stream of iron nails. As such it flows by rail to Southampton, thence via steamship along the ocean life-cord of the British Empire, through Gibraltar, Suez, Singapore to the gateway of Hong Kong; thence in streamlets to the hardware shops of China.

We might trace other streams—east and west, north and south; each rises in a field or mine or forest; each ends in a home; each passes en route through a series of converters (factories); each squeezes through bottle-necks (metropolises). (One fifth of America's export tonnage squeezes through the bottle-neck of New York harbor.)

Thus flows the Earthian blood system: silk pays for flour which pays for iron which pays for silk, *ad infinitum.* A marvelous creation! No more miraculous are the life processes of the human body than these on the surface of this cosmic cheese.

Alas! Like human life each such "cheese life" has but its single day. (So runs our theme of history.) A man's blood system is as old as its arteries. A planet's "blood system" is as old as its bottle-necks. And it suffers from the ills that we have mentioned—congestion, strikes, hard times. The streams get choked, or cease to flow, or otherwise run high and low—in spasm or depression.

Well, what of it? Should we mourn for the departing or prepare for the soul conceived? If one life system be in process of death why not another in process of birth? In simple cosmic perspective it would seem that if Earthians are doomed indeed to scrap their present set-up then it is in natural order to devise a substitute—to start afresh and chart the distribution of Earthly goods on a new pattern and technique. And a more efficient pattern. Chart the streams to flow directly, not (as now) in double crosses. Cancel out the cross-hauls. Spread the factories along the stream instead of huddling them. Reroute the streams to reduce the bottle-necks. Above all gauge each cargo by the demand at the stream's mouth, not (as now) by the supply at the stream's source.

"A Gargantuan order," you may call this. Not if we use well the Aladdin's lamps of our modern mechanical equipment. "A technique inexorably complex!" No more so than a dozen other techniques—in physics, mechanics, electrolysis.

In some such wise, then, would we act on civilization as a flow of the world's goods—and meet the challenge implied in the theme of Oswald Spengler.

The Flow of Folk

Next we shall accept the promise implied by Henry Adams which involves the problem of the flow of folk rather than of commodities and "things." The promise is indeed a possible solution of the growing issue between these two. Will folk control things—or things stampede folk? It depends on momentum. When a reservoir flows over, water and not man is temporary boss. As with water-flow so with commodity-flow—given enough momentum it controls the situation. While, as Henry Adams intimates, the power to make commodities shall *increase* (and accelerate), then the sheer force of productivity must push everything before it, and commodity not man obtain the right of way. But when, as also he implies, the course of productive power shall, like the comet's path, reverse itself—when it shall *decrease* (and decelerate)— then should man and not commodity control the day.

And so we hail the promise of the Adams theme: that industry (now wild) is going to be tamed by relieving its high tension at the source. Healthful relaxation of industry should release energy for culture. Or might it on the other hand lead to all-round indolence? In either case special effort would be due to culture—to stimulating ordered growth of human sensibilities. These sensibilities therefore we shall consider in this article, but we must vision first the folk movement of which they are a part. Let us then look at our American folk-flow; let us go upon another imaginary journey from the top of the Empire State Building.

America we saw, in our last journey, as one small blotch upon the globe—Europe another, China another. In our world survey of commodity-flow it was enough to trace a stream of silk from somewhere in China to somewhere in America; enough to trace a commodity-stream from somewhere in one country to somewhere in another. "Somewhere" was enough. A gray daub upon the globe indicated the population area of eastern United States; in world dimensions "Eastern U. S." is all one town within which the population is a fixture. But seen on closer view the constituent centers of said "Eastern U. S." are found to be not fixed but fluid. And if we traced commodity-flow within this area, from farm or mine to ultimate home, we should find that the latter itself is moving. This movement of the home is the ultimate *folk-flow*.

There have been three folk-flows, or migrations, in the land of America. First came the outward movement after 1776 when a population was led across a continent by the Covered Wagon. This, the agricultural migration, was followed after 1830 by the steam migration led by the Iron Horse. Following these tides—"Westward Ho!"—(and while they were still on) there developed, especially after 1880, the movement from the rural sections inward toward factory and skyscraper—toward the *city,* the *point* "in which the whole life of broad regions" was collecting.

These three folk-movements may be named in order: they are the outflow, the reflow, the inflow.

America is now in the midst of the fourth migration—
the *backflow*. This is the push from each central city backward toward the suburbs and beyond. The population of
the typical metropolis is flowing into the suburbs. (There
are plenty of figures to show this tendency.) It is flowing
farther—taking up its bungalow quarters along the motor
roads. This backflow is the vehicle for the *metropolitan
invasion* of America at large. We call it "invasion" because
it is in essence an intrusion—a malign intrusion—on the
innate American background. The intrusive taint attached to this particular folk-flow consists not in the city
folks themselves but in the metropolitan *environment*
which follows them.

The crudity and not the culture of the big city is what is
flowing to the outskirts and beyond. The crude massings
of suburban melancholy (the "Bronxes" and the "Hobo-
kens"), narrowing to "Motortowns" along the highways,
have now begun to ooze back toward the country in many
radiating streams.

The essential influence of these streams is now being
recognized under the precise and unexaggerated label,
"motor slum" (the name prescribed by Walter Prichard
Eaton). And so the big city, if menaced by a flood of
goods from outside sources, is itself the source and menace
of another kind of flood invading the outer stretches of
America.

And this brings us to the human sensibilities involved
in America's folk-flow.

Human Considerations

Destiny vs. destination. This is the distinction between
the objectives sought in the guidance respectively of folk-
flow and of commodity-flow. With the latter the final

goal is the delivery of worldly goods at the consumer's home, wherever this happens to be. With the former the goal consists in providing the home itself, and the home community. Each of the American folk-flows cited—outflow, reflow, inflow, backflow—is (or was) a quest for a better state in human living. This better state consists of two things—a better job and a better home. A better home consists of a better house and a better community, and the second is fundamental to the first. Social environment is basic to individual; and failure to perceive this truth is one big cause of failure by the individual to improve his lot. Commodity-flow is concerned with physical destination; folk-flow with social destiny.

Destiny has its inner and its outer aspects. We deal here with the outer aspects, the "geography" so to speak of human betterment. The influence of this geography affects of course the inner mind: this influence is indeed the *common mind* shared by our inmost selves. Air is the common substance of our physical breath. Environment is the common substance of our total human life; the biologist calls it the "sum total of influences affecting an organism from without." Only by bettering this "sum total" can we better our own lives.

"To carve the very atmosphere through which we look" —this, says Thoreau, is "the highest of arts."

What manner of "atmosphere" (environment) is required for human betterment? There seem to be three kinds whose proper balance is innate in permanent human welfare:

1. The *primeval* environment, from which we sprung.

2. The *communal* environment, in which we grew up as social beings.

3. The *rural* environment, which bridges the other two.

They are the settings respectively of forest, village, field. They form the background of all human life; combined they make that basic native innate influence which we shall call the *indigenous* environment; against this any other type comes as an *intrusive* influence. This indigenous environment, in final analysis, forms the source of mental life and culture—even as the Earth itself is the source of material life and industry. As we maintain industry by conserving the natural resources of soil and wood and waterpower, so we maintain culture by developing the "natural resource" of innate environment. And the true city (the grown-up village) is part of this resource.

But not the pseudo-city called "metropolis": its environment is intrusive, not innate; it is a massing not a unit, a collection not a community, an inorganic deposit not an organism. The metropolis is the source of the "metropolitan invasion"—that intrusive slum environment which is fastening its grip on the backflow of population. This backflow even now is moulding the American future. Through it one influence or the other must pervade our future town and countryside—the intrusive, or the indigenous (as above defined). The metropolitan forces, blind but powerful, are working for the first; certain American forces, gradually becoming conscious, are working for the second. The latter are proceeding on three separate but related lines of action:

1.   Retention of the wilderness stretches along the mountain ranges and elsewhere, thereby preserving the primeval environment. (The conservation movement.)

2.   Guidance of the backflow to make not massings but communities, thereby conserving the communal environment. (The town planning movement.)

3.   Clearance from the highways of the motor slum,

thereby maintaining the rural environment. (The highway reform movement.)

In such ways, then, would we act on civilization as a flow of American folk—we would control said flow to preserve that innate native environment which forms the base of native culture: so to greet the promise of that more enlightened day implied in the theme of Henry Adams.

We return finally to the Empire State Building. We have been on two journeys, one above the Earth, the other above America. We have surveyed the problem of commodity-flow—that of physical destination, of making a living throughout the world. We have surveyed the matter of folk-flow—the geography of social destiny in one place in the world. These are pictures which loom from the American metropolis. One arises from that flood of goods pressing on the city's gates; the other from that backflow which itself is causing flood beyond the gates. Each depicts a *city* problem—one incoming, one outgoing.

What means it all, the end or the peak of modern civilization? Nobody knows. What then? Prepare for both, meet the challenge of the one, greet the promise of the other.

IO.

Tennessee—Seed of a National Plan

Muscle Shoals—to be or not to be publicly operated? That was the question. That *is* the question, yet unanswered, before Congress. The question has been sharpened by President Roosevelt's proposed development of the Tennessee River Valley: shall a public concern (the United States government) do the job for public service, or a private concern (a power company) do the job for private profit? The same old question. But it is broadened as well as sharpened. President Roosevelt has spread it out from a dam to a river to a region; from the Muscle Shoals dam to the Tennessee River to the Appalachian Region. He has done more—he has related a local project to a national emergency; he has sown the seed of that "national planning" announced in his inauguration speech.

It is a good place to begin, the old Tennessee Valley. It was where Daniel Boone began; where the first march "Westward Ho!" began—right there through the Watauga River, one of the upper branches of the Tennessee. I used to think of Daniel in my younger days when, back in 1908, as a government forester under Gifford Pinchot and

Reprinted from *Survey Graphic,* Vol. XXII, No. 5 (May, 1933), pp. 251-54, 293-94.

President "T.R.," I was sent into those self-same upper branches to study the forest growth on their steep eroding slopes. And now that I'm a generation older I'll dare divulge, in strictest confidence, how in those blossoming June days I did at times dismount my Dobbin in some strategic gap and, climbing up among the luxuriant hardwoods, would in pretense shade my eyes and focus them on the serene bottomlands below, wondering whether Daniel himself ever looked on them thus while entering his promised continent. And I could pause right here and tell you wondrous tales of the gentle, self-lawed folks hoeing their hillside cornfields under the "deadenings" or sitting by twilight on the veranda above the wallowing razorback.

"What happened to the sun the other day?" once

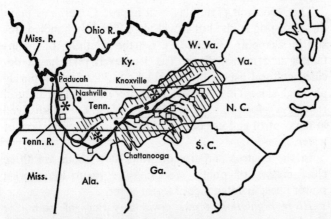

The Tennessee Valley plan for control and use of water flow. The boxes mark river regulation works, dams and reservoirs; the stars indicate power lines to distribute current; and the shaded areas show forest cover on slopes. Muscle Shoals Dam is at the large circle. Maps by the author.

drawled my host on such a twilight spot, about three nights after a solar eclipse.

I explained according to Copernicus and the Red Schoolhouse geography. Host looked blank and with exquisite tact refrained from open argument.

"Right smart distance to the sun, I suppose?"

"Right smart," I answered to his lead.

"Well," says he, coming to the point, "the *Bible* says there's four corners of the earth and an angel at each corner"—this spoken with a clinching air of gravity that woke me up.

"I see," says I, "you don't agree with this notion that the earth is round; apparently you believe that it's *flat*."

"Well, I'm bound to say it's flat in every place that *I* ever was!"

And so he won.

The Roosevelt plan, alas, will impose Copernicus upon these trusting souls; but it will also, if rightly handled, result in swapping the cultures, not the crudities, of mountaineer and metropolitan. The Roosevelt plan has a decided cultural aspect but we shall consider first its purely physical side. This consists in conserving certain natural resources—forests, soils, waters; and these are all involved in the control and use of one of them—namely, the flow of *water*.

In the control and use of water flow there are three chief classes of public works: river regulation works; power lines; maintenance of forest cover.

River regulation works cover a variety of plans for checking the stream's flow and holding it in bounds. The storage reservoir is the basic means: this stores the flood and lets it out again in a steady level from one peak to the next; the storage at Muscle Shoals makes only one in a string of storages; most of these are planned for the headwater valleys—the Hiwassee, the Little Tennessee, the Pigeon, the French Broad, the upper Holston. With reservoirs upstream go levees and revetment works downstream, holding the water in its channel. The river is an individual with a behavior of its own; its control is a whole technology.

Power lines are in effect extensions of the rivers wherein the flow, converted into electric juice, moves on through copper wires from power-plant to smokeless factory and home. The location of new power lines therefore involves the larger problem of locating the towns to be supplied. These towns would of course be down in the valley bottoms and not up on the mountains; and we shall return to this important part of civilization-building.

Forest cover is needed however up on the mountain slopes, there to hold in check the headwater streams and act as sponge in absorbing the pelting rains; forest cover is indeed a sort of giant's doormat flung athwart the mountain, a natural reservoir above the man-made kind.

All three means (river works, power lines, forest maintenance) require their measure of labor, and President Roosevelt thereby hopes to set at work many thousands of men. Well, that depends upon how far he and Congress care to go. And right here is a practical point to bear in mind: that forest work gives more jobs, per money expended, than building dams or power lines.

Forest jobs are of various kinds. Of course there's tree planting (though many gaps should be reforested by natural seeding). But quite as important as forest planting is forest *thinning*. This aids the fittest trees in their survival and "fattens" them for final crops, and the whole Eastern forest should have a wholesale thinning. There's work enough in the forests alone to give jobs to all the men whose physical sustenance Congress would pay for. For it is work of a prehistoric type: the human engine (aided by ax and horse) does the bulk of the operation; the lumberjack is one last man of flesh and blood whose job has not been seized by the iron man of mechanism.

Some interesting figures on this point occur in a recent comparison made of employment available per $100 expenditure, between forest and construction work. For every man-day needed on a certain California aqueduct, forest work (all kinds averaged) would require 5.75 man-days; forest improvement (fire protection, thinnings) would need 6.50 man-days; and forest planting, 10.85 man-days. So here, back in the woods, is the place if any to absorb the present unemployed, and this indeed is slowly being done in the public forests within the Appalachian domain.

There is another practical point to bear in mind. It applies especially to power lines and the town-building which naturally goes with them. Question, is this dream of President Roosevelt to come true in a piece of true statescraft —or in one more real-estate adventure? Is the word "Tennessee" to join company with "Florida"? How about it, Mr. President? Speculation is all it will amount to unless you take special measures to prevent it.

The Appalachian Valleys

So much for the Tennessee Valley project. But President Roosevelt hints at something further—that Tennessee is but the seed. After all Mr. Roosevelt is president of something more extensive than the Tennessee Valley. He says the scheme would apply in other valleys. It surely would; and some fifteen others are at hand through the Appalachian Mountain region—the Kanawah, James, Shenandoah, Susquehanna, Delaware, Hudson, Connecticut and several more.

Each of these valleys repeats the need toward waters, power, forests. Witness New England's great flood of November, 1927; witness the cry of her folks for cheap electric juice (to catch up with their neighbors over in Canada); witness her forests, more depleted than those on the southern crests. Yet this array of Appalachian valleys em-

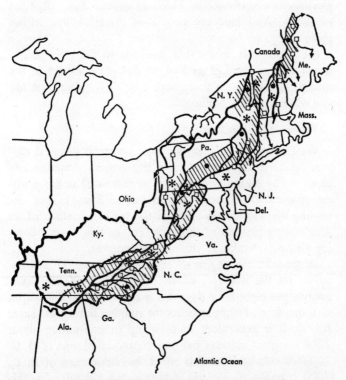

How water flow might be controlled and used in all the Appalachain valleys as in the plan for the Tennessee River valley. The shaded areas are sources of water. The small arrows point the trend of the flow. The boxes mark river regulation works, the stars indicate power lines in the lower valleys, and the dots show forest cover on mountain slopes.

braces a physical empire whose power in terms of natural resources is second to none on earth. These valleys taken together rival the whole continent of Europe—both in bulk and in balance found of iron, coal and waterpower, of soils and *latent* forest growth. The mountains, forests, fields of this Appalachian country make it one of the most glorious *environments* in which to restore the exiled art of living. And half the people of America live within these valleys or close by.

Mr. Roosevelt relates his program to the present national emergency. Let us look at this grave aspect of the matter. Let us ask (along with Lincoln) "where we are and whither we are tending?"

Where and Whither

We of America live in the most powerful physical empire on earth; and we of twentieth-century America live in what (by measurement if not appearance) is the greatest physical culmination yet in human history (not excepting the Flood). We live in the top-notch stage of an accelerating process of industry. To see this, take a fleeting glance at mankind's engineering progress.

Begin with the engine of the human body. This is capable, on the average, of an output of 1,500,000 footpounds per eight-hour day; this is equivalent to the output of a one tenth horsepower motor running during the same period; it is equivalent to using up or consuming about 2000 kilogram calories per day. Neanderthal man of B. C. 200,000 subsisted on this effort. Neolithic man of B. C. 7000 brought to his aid domesticated animals: by this means, plus soil culture and crude uses of fire, he made available about double the energy at the command of man unaided (or about 4000 kilogram calories per day). Roughly speaking this was the ration also of the average

Roman living in A. D. 1 and of the average American in 1776.

Since about 1830 the daily ration of energy at the command of the average American has increased on account of the development of a new extraneous means of living, namely the harnessing of the energy of coal, oil, water-power and other inorganic resources through steam and electric machinery. Thereby the daily per capita energy ration has increased about as follows:

1830	2,600 kilogram calories
1880	30,000 " "
1900	72,300 " "
1929	154,000 " "

The above figures are given through the courtesy and permission of *Technocracy*. According to them, modern mechanical power could hand out to Mr. Average American today seventy-seven times the energy ration of un-aided prehistoric man; or thirty-eight times the ration of crudely aided historic man; or more than twice the ration of ourselves a generation ago (in 1900). Such is "the Flood" of modern power.

So here is *where* we seem to be: in an empire second to none on earth; in a stage of mechanical power wholly foreign to all past history. *Whither* are we tending?

Less Work—More Leisure

Whatever else the future holds for us, a redistribution of activity seems to be among the items—less work and more leisure. What else can we expect from an industrial mechanism which increases, seventy-seven times over, a man's capacity for doing work? Right now a quarter of America's population is—pitiably and tragically—placed within a "leisure class"; and more than half of their one-time normal jobs (55 per cent) would now, even under total business revival, be taken by machines, not men. No, this spells not the world's end. Rationality in time must somehow come; men be placed at part-time labor; paid with the lavish gifts of power; and thus comfort, not destitution, become the running-mate of leisure.

But this alone would not spell the world's redemption.

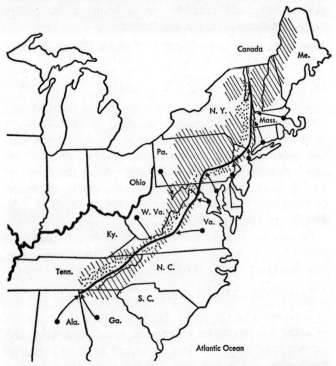

How population flow might be controlled in the Appalachian valleys. The big dots are principal cities—sources of the "backflow" of population. The arrows show the trend, via highway. The means of control are a townless highway to connect the valleys (as shown), highwayless towns (shown by small dots), and wilderness to be reserved on the slopes (shaded areas).

Culture beside comfort must be added if we would still escape perdition. Man lives not by bread alone, nor by clothing, nor by shelter: a fourth ingredient is needed— a thing called *environment*. What coal and soil and timber are to industry so environment is to culture—the source from which it springs. If we are tending toward leisure, then half the task of statesmanship is to stimulate our culture. To preserve the source thereof (within our dwelling-place and land) is half the task of public works.

Don't confuse environment with beauty: don't confuse the total source with any part thereof. Environment is outward influence; it is literal and mental atmosphere; it is a permeating medium of life. This medium is pliable: it can be molded toward definite goals: toward safety of surroundings; toward salubrity of temperature; toward presence of the beautiful in nature, man, and both. It can be purged of definite defects: of disease germs, baneful odors, hideous sights, jarring sounds. Environment may be likened to the spectrum: with safety at one end and beauty at the other; with the salubrious and the healthful in between.

Three environments stand forth as fundamental to our needs—the primeval, the communal, and the rural. Each is an elemental presence; each appeals to all of human kind; each is the source of a special outdoor culture embodied respectively in forest, home, and wayside. A fourth environment stands forth as the negation of the elemental—an influence intrusive upon the native base: I refer to the commercial or metropolitan *slum*. This slum is the product largely of accelerated power; it invades the sources of our culture (forest, home, wayside).

We are tending toward leisure with the sources of culture threatened; we have arrived at a leisure acute with destitution.

What then to do? Relieve the present and protect the future. Such in two words seems to be Mr. Roosevelt's program. Its application in the Tennessee Valley can be repeated in other valleys; Tennessee is but the gate to the Appalachian country. The control and use of the flow of water makes, as we have seen, the physical portion of the program. This is the base for the cultural portion—the conservation of the basic settings (of wilderness, community, wayside) and their protection from the influx of the metropolitan slum. In short, to conserve the basic cultural settings we must control the flow of the metropolis.

Control of Population Flow

So we pass from the flow of water to that of population. The *river* is the guide in one, the *highway* in the other. The highway is to 1933 what the railway was to 1833— the framework of a civilization. Let us see how this came to be.

Return to 1776. The average American of that day, like the Egyptian and the Neolithic, subsisted, as we have seen, on a daily energy ration of 4000 kilogram calories; and likewise with our own great-grandpapa of 1833, driving his oxen in front of the Covered Wagon which led the first American migration across the continent. Enter now (in the 1830's) the Iron Horse, beginning to replace the Covered Wagon; enter therewith the steam age with its higher daily energy ration; enter also the second American migration—a factory migration on top of the agrarian— a *reflow* of the population on the new technical basis.

Jump now to 1900. The growth of the new technique has made a whirlpool around the factory and skyscraper; and a third migration has now got going—the *inflow* of the population sucking in from the rural areas toward the urban centers. As streams of water flow in to the millpond and push against the dam, so with inflow of population against the factory and office building: in each case a tidal movement pushes back "upstream." This *backflow* of the population makes the fourth American migration—today's. The backflow is the movement back into the suburbs and beyond; it is the invasion of the hinterland by the metropolitan slum.

Compare the sources of our "flows." The mountain forest is the source of the flow of water along the river; the metropolis is the source of the "backflow" along the highway. The Appalachian valleys (especially those between the Tennessee and the Hudson) lie in the wake of the backflows from all the big eastern centers. To handle these backflows within these valleys is the major task of planning in this region. Indeed the inter-mountain lane formed by these valleys (from Lake Champlain to Tennessee) is perhaps the most strategic line for guiding the present or fourth American migration and for molding the country's future. Governor Al Smith has suggested having a dictator of public works. If I were given the job I'd build a specially constructed highway through this inter-mountain lane from one end to the other. Its purpose would be to hold in check the "flood" of population from the cities (even as the river holds in check a flood of waters from the mountains).

The Townless Highway

It takes a special kind of highway to hold this flood in check. Elsewhere I have described it. I've called it a "townless highway" (it would as far as possible avoid passing through the towns). Another name is "insulated highway," and still another is "cement railroad" (see *Survey Graphic* for November, 1932). Its major design is nothing more nor less than the pattern of a railroad: establish stations for entrance and departure where gas and food and every traveler's whim is to be served; then close the road *between* the stations to entrance, parking, exit.

The essence of the pattern is *inaccessibility*. Edward Bassett gives a well chosen name to the inter-station stretch: he calls it a "freeway." To make its meaning clear he defines it side by side with two other concepts with which it is continually confused. Here they are:

A "highway" is a strip of public land devoted to *movement* over which the abutting property owners have the right of light, air and access.

A "parkway" is a strip of public land devoted to *recreation* over which the abutting property owners have *no* right of light, air or access.

A "freeway" is a strip of public land devoted to *movement* over which the abutting property owners have *no* right of light, air or access.

Thus the freeway, by excluding abutting property owners, makes it automatically pointless to erect buildings of any sort beside the way. This means that the freeway must acquire its own right-of-way, since to improve an old highway and then try to exclude the abutting owners would usually precipitate a hornet's nest of litigation. The freeway automatically kills the motor slum and (especially if double-tracked) cuts down the chance of accident; it creates an environment of automatic safety along with one of spontaneous rural wayside beauty.

But what becomes of "the Flood"—the *substance* of the motor slum? We can keep the traffic moving, but development and building must somewhere settle down. Then where? If not on the freeway stretches then how about the "stations"? No, not there except in small degree, as needed by the travelers. For this is a *townless* highway. This brings us to the next step in controlling the flow of population.

Highwayless Towns

It is just as important to keep the town off the highway as to keep the highway out of the town. And here again we have a pattern which points a principle: this exists in solid structure in the town of Radburn, New Jersey (out near Paterson) planned and built by the City Housing Corporation. Radburn is called the "town for the motor age": it is the living divorce of dwelling and transport. It consists of a series of pockets, cells, or cul-de-sacs. Each cul-de-sac consists of a dead-end street leading off a main street; the dead-end street is lined with houses back of which is park area totally inaccessible by motor-car; the dead-end street automatically eliminates all traffic except that destined for its houses; pedestrians move throughout the town via paths passing through the park areas and below (or above) the main streets; thus the medium of the pedestrian and that of the motor-car are as distinct as the media of land and water.

As dictator of public works I should extend this scheme to laying out my highwayless towns. What the cul-de-sac is to the main street my whole town would be to my through (townless) highway; spur-roads would lead off from the stations ending (at substantial distances) in single towns. What the cul-de-sac is to the town of Radburn my whole town would be to its surrounding region—*with this exception:* that I would as far as possible fix the limits of my town and surround it by substantial open areas.

The town as a whole must be divorced from through-line transport, but something more is needed for it to be a real community. This something is *individuality*—which is the essence of community environment; hence the need of the surrounding open areas. Thus would we preserve community integrity against an endless, wormlike "roadtown" on the one hand and against a sprawling sea of suburbs on the other. Here then we "pool the flood" and change it from a slum into an environment of safety, beauty, and communal consciousness.

A Forest Wilderness

So much for the town, how about the wilderness? The primeval influence (as well as the communal) is basic to our human needs; and here again the chief invader is the uncontrolled highway. As in the town so in the forest the primal means of movement is the foot; and a comprehensive footpath system (the Appalachian Trail) is being now completed through the mountain forest wilderness from Maine to Georgia. With forest as with town (especially the mountain forest) the chief function of the motor-car is to deliver, not to enter. Exceptions are evident, especially across the gaps and even to the tops of certain peaks. But the arch intruder of the mountain fastness is the "skyline drive." This cuts the wilderness in two: the skyline marks the backbone of both range and wilderness belt, hence the skyline road splits the belt in halves. Skyline is to sky what coastline is to sea: each is the meeting-place of two terrestrial elements. The panoramic view therefore is a topnotched experience and, like all superlatives in life, is truly absorbed by occasional exercise; it is merely dulled by repetition, such as on the skyline drive.

Of opposite effect to the skyline type is the lateral mountain drive. This flanks the range instead of topping it. It follows the base and sides, passing through gaps from one flank to the other—and across an *occasional* summit. Such a drive ensconced on the sides, sights more actual scenery than one parading on the skyline. One sees up the slope and down better than from the skyline—as well as off and away, with view changing at each turn. A case in point is the drive leading eastward from Bear Mountain Bridge in the Hudson Highlands. My townless highway along the inter-mountain lane would indeed be such a lateral mountain drive and act as substitute for any future contemplated drives upon the skyline.

Instead of a Pacific Railroad

These three developments of townless highway, of highwayless town, of forest wilderness, I would, as public works dictator, place side by side in one long belt connecting the Appalachian valleys. The heart of this triple project is the highway. Highways are to this century what railways were to the last: an Appalachian highway instead of a Pacific railway. And each is (or was) something more than a roadbed.

The Pacific Railroad was a land grant as well as a roadbed; alternate sections of public land were deeded to the enterprise, these covering belts on each side of the track twenty or forty miles in width. This belt made the backbone of the second American migration across the western states (what we've called the "reflow"). If today we had a public domain and the government granted to a townless highway scheme a series of town-sites instead of alternate sections, then such a belt would make the backbone for guiding the fourth American migration (what we've called the "backflow"). Alas, the public domain is no more, but the government (state or federal) can still grant rights-of-way; and public forests can be purchased (as already in the Appalachians); and town sites can be acquired (as at Radburn).

The Tennessee Valley project sows the seed of a national plan for the country's redevelopment. The control and use of water flow within said valley spreads inevitably to those adjoining; control of water flow begets control of population flow, and the regulated river begets the regulated highway. Within a day's ride of the Appalachian valleys live half the people of America. Further steps—in the Mississippi valleys and beyond—where the other half of America lives—must in due course carry on the national evolution conceived in the Roosevelt statesmanship.

II.

Region Building in River Valleys

Upstream Community vs. Downstream Slum

Region building is the enlightened regulation of regional activity or "flow." There are three main types: the flow of *waters* via the regional river system or watershed; the flow of *commodities* via river, road, and rail; the flow of folks themselves or *population* in their various migrations.

These three flows (of waters, things, folks) combine in various ways. One critical combination is that of water and of folks. These two meet in the common problem of what to do about our towns and cities seated within our flood plains. Here housing and river control appear to coincide in a striking illustration of their interdependence and of the choice of kind of planning—whether (1) to conserve existing flood-menaced slums at enormous money cost and at the cost of flooding sound upstream communities by dam building; or whether (2) at much less money cost, human cost and cost of disarranging nature's proceedings, we should let the urban flood-slum areas disappear, and conserve and build up our natural and human resources upstream.

Reprinted from *Survey Graphic,* Vol. XXIX, No. 2 (Feb., 1940), pp. 106-8.

The typical American city, large or small, tends to be an unformed mass and not a balanced, bounded, separate community organism. It tends thus to develop cancerous tissue; this is seen in the typical inchoate suburban masses and their pseudopodic extensions along the radiating highways—the well known "motor slums."

Besides this cancerous tissue, which tends to *run wild*, the typical mass city contains areas tending to *run down*.

These two kinds of slums—the decaying tissue, or blight, or slum, in the center and cancerous growths on the outskirts—are the twin results of any community gone diseased from the loss of normal balance and control.

A flood plain is part of the fluvial anatomy—an upper-level channel reserved by nature for the region's stormy periods and seasons. Water, then, has first right to the flood plains. All other would-be occupants are trespassers; they sojourn at their own risk and subject to the primary overlord. Hay can be cut and cattle pastured and even corn grown and harvested; also folks may play baseball or stage a Sunday school picnic; but here is no place for barns or sheds or factories, and least of all for homes. Housing of whatever form has no place upon the stream's domain—except at terrific risk and huge costs.

American river-cities are essentially trespassing cities —every last one of them from Pittsburgh to New Orleans. True, their flood plains were the handiest place to settle originally. But a couple of tools invented since have reduced to the minimum the need for hanging around the water fronts: one is the electric power line; another is the motor car.

But we have vested property interests in the mud—and these in turn breed wage interests. So here we stick— snugly and smugly—'til Old Man River decides on some dark and stormy night to resume his ancient and honorable and inevitable riparian rights. Then we rush around and cry "catastrophe"!

But we trespassers, not the elements, cause the human catastrophe. With proper and legitimate town building "floods" would seldom bother us.

Trespassers on the Flood Plain

Prominent among flood plain trespassers is the slum. The flood plain slum therefore is an element common to our two problems: it is part of the housing problem—the part called slum clearance; it also figures in river control. "Flood plain slum clearance" we might call it. Its prosecution would aid in two directions: toward better housing and town building; toward better flood control.

Housing is one of the keys to region building; as such it deals with one of the regional flows—that of the folks themselves; and is a guide to folk flow—toward the suburbs from the city on the one side and from the country on the other.

The suburbs we may compare to a glacier whose movement on the whole is away from the center and along the radiating lanes. Can its "flow" or "growth" be guided even further backward toward the open? Can it be molded into healthful forms—not those of the motor slum or wayside sprawl?

One approach toward bringing this to pass is that of clearing the slum. This requires that for every slum cleared a community must somewhere be created. The process is a double one—clearance in one place and creation in another. One place for clearance is within the river city.

Flood control as well as housing is a key to region building; it also deals with one of the regional flows—that of water. For this it requires knowledge of fluvial tendencies and laws—specifically of stream behavior and movements.

Two primary methods of dealing with stream movements may be cited:

1. To let the river flow its natural way and refrain from trespassing upon its rightful path. This means occasional downstream flooding of its flood plain.

2. To restrict the natural downstream flooding by means of artificial upstream flooding (and allied operations). Usually this means permanent appropriation for water storage purposes of upstream farm lands with their buildings, roads and towns.

Property owners are involved at both ends—the farmer whose lands occupy a potential storage space upstream, and the city man whose lands occupy parts of the flood plain downstream. Question then—to what extent are we warranted in robbing an Upstream "Peter" in order to pay a Downstream "Paul"?

In order to keep things simple suppose that Peter, together with his neighbors, owns *all* the land and property upstream within the potential water storage reservoir; and that Paul, together with his business associates, owns *all* the land and property downstream on the flood plain which the proposed upstream storage would protect. Each puts in his bill for damages.

Such bills bring up imposing questions: How shall such damages be appraised? In what unit can they truthfully be measured? In dollars merely or in some unit more realistic?

Consider first the *dollar*. Flood damages to the downstream flood plain property of "Paul & Co." amount in the course of time to $1,000,000 per year. A reservoir located on the upstream land of Peter and his neighbors would store enough water to reduce Paul's downstream damages by $475,000 per year. (This sum is known as *annual benefits*). The value of Peter's upstream land and property amounts to an annual charge of $250,000, and the annual charge for the reservoir itself is $200,000. The sum of these ($450,000) makes the total *annual costs*. If *benefits* exceed *costs,* it is argued the reservoir must be built. In this case benefits *are* in excess of costs ($475,000 exceeds $450,000). Therefore—Peter's upstream property must be flooded and Paul's downstream property saved Q.E.D.

Well, is this all there is to it? If it came to a showdown ought we in truth to sacrifice Peter's upstream home—and perhaps a community of homes—in order to save Paul's downstream slum?

Let us see what Uncle Sam has to say about it. Read Section 1 of the present flood control law, the act signed by President Roosevelt on June 22, 1936. Here are the first words:

"It is hereby recognized that destructive floods upon the rivers of the United States . . . constitute a menace to national welfare; that it is the sense of Congress . . . that the federal government should . . . participate in the improvement of navigable waters or their tributaries, including watersheds thereof, for flood control purposes if the benefits to whomsoever they may accrue are in excess of the estimated costs, and if the lives and social security of people are otherwise adversely affected."

Let us list some possible terms (or units) in which we may, by implication at least, construe this concisely stated *bill of flood rights*. First of all it is clear that we may construe it in terms of "national welfare"—also in terms of "lives of people," and of their "social security." This being so, may not *benefits* be measured in such terms as well as in terms of money? And the same with *costs?* With this construction in mind let us look once more at the case of Peter vs. Paul.

Again to make things simple, and to bring out a principle, let us assume a deliberately exaggerated case: Suppose the upstream lands and homes of Peter and his neighbors constitute what has been alluded to in this article as a true *community*—a social geographic unit, or organism, properly located and recognized as a normal and healthful form and mode of living in America. Suppose the downstream lands and property of Paul & Co. constitute a *slum* —an area of social decay.

Which *ought* to be flooded—Peter's upstream *community* or Paul's downstream *slum?*

Measured in terms of money values, as above cited, Peter's community *ought* to be erased and Paul's slum maintained. Because the money benefits are in excess of the money costs.

Measured in terms of American "national welfare," in the "lives of people," or in their "social security"—which area ought to be maintained—upstream community or downstream slum? Though the answer appears obvious we have no "arithmetic" for demonstrating it; and have been losing by default for the lack of a device.

According to money values, Paul's slum wins. According to human welfare values, Peter's community should win. Here arises a profound question—*how to value values?*

On the assumption of relative human values, flood control should in most cases begin *downstream* instead of upstream. The intrinsic social worth of downstream property should first be studied to determine which of it is, and which is not, located to deserve legitimate protection. This *first* step in sane flood control means for one thing the elimination of flood plain slum areas as legitimate objects of protection. This step once taken, the means of securing protection for the legitimate areas—and no others —should then be sought *upstream*. This is the *second* step of any sane flood control.

Land Hygiene vs. Land Surgery

While the river's habitat or watershed retains its natural covering—whether of forest or grass or other protecting vegetative growth—the flow of water draining therefrom is sufficiently retarded to hold the river, even in high water, within the rightful flood plain which experience through the ages has found sufficient for normal flooding. But the trouble is that American watersheds possess no longer their complete natural covering.

The big job to be done *upstream* is to practice scientific forest using and scientific grass and soil using, cease ruining the soil, and by crop rotation and contour planting, practice treatment of the land to heal its scars and restore its coverage—in other words, practice *land hygiene*.

This is a long job. For the farmers and folks on the watershed must be "sold" to the big idea. All this takes time —time measured in years and decades. Meanwhile the land scars stay unhealed and the water and silt flow on unretarded. Can anything on earth be done in order to retard them soon—this year or next? Yes, we can build dams and thereby make storage pools or reservoirs. This will check abnormal flowage till long time retardation can set in. In other words, practice *land surgery* till land hygiene has had time to work.

Both of these lines of work—the surgical or structural operations, and the hygiene or cultural operations—once systematically and substantially prosecuted on the upstream section of a watershed, would amount to a redevelopment of the headwaters area.

Thus the lumber cut each year would be reduced to the growth each year; cattle on the hoof would be reduced in numbers to retain a grass sod which would support a steady yield of milk and beef; electric power generated in modest voltage from obscure and minor dams could turn the wheels of obscure but efficient smokeless factories. Such slow but sure economy, based on up-to-date machinery, might well become the basis of a series of small unobtrusive and truly livable communities into which the "backflow" of population might be guided.

And a natural part of such a redevelopment would be the side partner of slum clearance—namely community building.

Every slum cleared, as we have said, requires a community created. Suppose 1000 inhabitants of a flood plain slum are deliberately "dehoused"; then somewhere else they must be as deliberately "rehoused." One way to do this is to build somewhere a new community of 1000 persons capacity. This does not mean that each inhabitant of the slum would be lifted by the ear and deposited in the new community. But since in this case the minus housing occurs downstream the plus housing could appropriately be encouraged to occur upstream—as part of the redevelopment of the headwater area.

Note what Congress writes in the last flood control law —the act of June 28, 1938.

"MINUS HOUSING"

Thus Section 3 of the act reads as follows concerning *evacuation:*

"That in any case where the construction cost of levees or flood walls included in any authorized project can be substantially reduced by the evacuation of . . . the area proposed to be protected and by the elimination of that . . . area from the protection to be afforded by the proj-

ect, the chief of engineers may modify the plan of said
project so as to eliminate . . . the area. . . ."

"PLUS HOUSING"

Section 3 reads as follows concerning *rehabilitation:*
"Provided, That a sum not substantially exceeding the
amount thus saved in construction cost may be expended
by the chief of engineers . . . toward the evacuation of
the locality eliminated from protection and the rehabilitation of the persons so evacuated. . . ."

This is the first congressional sanction looking toward
a new and enlightened approach to the whole problem of
flood control—that of protecting area and property on
the basis of their legitimate relation to the required path of
the river.

Neither Rome nor Region is built in a day. It is earth we
want, not heaven. Our objective is a habitable abode—a
place, as Sir Raymond Unwin says, of "pleasant living and
convenient work." Our method is one of directing tendencies and flows—whether of river or folk.

Before direction comes study, and before study comes
a clear vision of objectives. Objectives are the outcome of
a sense of values: is it wealth we value or welfare—is it
the status of a bad investment or the pursuit of happiness?

These are idle questions till occasion gives them life.
Too often this must be a calamitous occasion—like the
wartime evacuations in England, which are bound to
make permanent some of the hitherto impossible dreams
of the planners. As with war, so with floods: evacuation
from the scene of action may become an immediate and
absolute necessity; and then it is not enough that people
should have been taken to safety. They must have a
chance to live their lives completely—in the more sensible
communities which should evolve.

part III

Uses
of the Wilderness

12.

A New England
Recreation Plan*

A plan is a picture—a visualization of some scheme. To
be effective it must be nature's scheme—not man's. Planning is exploration. The civil engineer who plans an effective railway grade across a mountain range does not
devise the grade, he finds it. He finds the line of least
resistance in nature's topographic scheme. He reveals
the setting for some activity. The railway grade is the setting for the activity of transportation. Transportation is a
regional activity; so is agriculture; so is manufacturing.
These form the industrial half of man's activity; recreation of some kind forms the other half. A plan for a region
is the revelation of nature's setting for some activity.

Before exploring for the setting we first must know
what activity is called for. Is it industry or recreation? Is it
work or is it play? It must be one or the other, even though
the two may be combined. We must know the objectives
of each in order to provide that they will not conflict with
one another. Also we must know the means for achieving
the various objectives. These statements are platitudes,

Reprinted from *Journal of Forestry*, Vol. XXVII, No. 8 (Dec.,
1929), pp. 927-30.
* Presented at the Third New England Forestry Congress, Hart-
ford, Conn., Feb. 2, 1929.

but engineering is based on platitudes—precise, however, not vague. Let us get our platitudes precise.

Industry is necessary for bodily existence. Its objectives are finite—food, clothing, houses, etc. And the ability to secure these objectives as efficiently as possible is itself an objective of industry. The less time spent in drudging to secure the means for mere existence the more time we have left to use these means for actual living. These objectives are finite and commonplace, but they are sublime. The means of industry consist of various forms and processes—thousands of them; we can dispose of them under the single word *mechanism*.

Recreation is not necessary for bodily existence (except a certain minimum), but it *is* necessary for real living. Recreation is not merely "non-industry," it is the reason for industry. Industry provides existence which is the base for living. Recreation is incipient culture—the final lap in the pursuit of happiness. Its objectives are not finite, they are infinite. They are the mysteries and the melodies of creation; they are pursued through science and art. The means of recreation and culture consist, as with industry, of various forms and processes; these we can dispose of under the single word *technique*.

Means and ends! To confuse these is the worst mistake that a planner can make—or the citizen either. Yet this is just what most citizens are usually doing. And this is why we must be precise about our platitudes. To worship any means for its own sake is fruitless, pointless, and too often disastrous. To worship technique for technique's sake—the forms and fashions of art—leads to nothing but a foppish cult barren of the basic vital interests of life. This is what the "transcendentalists" were supposed to be doing in England back in the mid-Victorian days when they were spanked warmly by the satire of Gilbert and Sullivan in that display of real art—the comic opera *Patience*. Equally barren is the mechanistic cult—born of the worship of the forms and fashions of industry. I refer to the present-day madness for instrumentalities—the radio, the moving picture, the high-powered motor car, and the other push-button fixtures of mechanistic civilization. In these cases there seems to be a tendency for mechanistic motion to be worshipped for its own sake.

There are two kinds of motions or movements in the world—the kind which counts and the kind which does not. The game of football illustrates both kinds. Forward movement down the field in the direction of the goal is the kind that counts. Lateral movement across the field between the yard lines does not count because the ball is no nearer the goal at the end of such movement than it was at the beginning. As with football so with life—our movement or activity is forward and fruitful or else it is lateral and fruitless. The difference may be further illustrated in two stories.

In *Through the Looking-Glass* one of the adventures takes place with a character known as the "Black Queen." This lady, seizing Alice by the hand, bids her to run with her as fast as she can. They start. "Faster, faster!" shouts the Black Queen. Alice goes into higher speed. "Faster, faster!" again shouts the Black Queen. Alice puts on full power. Suddenly both drop exhausted under a tree. "Where are we now?" gasps poor little Alice between her heart throbs. "Just where we were before," pants the Black Queen.

In a recent reminiscence of Henry David Thoreau a certain old farmer, after explaining that Thoreau's real name was "Da-a-vid Henry," gives the following description:

One morning I went out in my field across there to the river, and there, beside that little old mud pond, was standin' Da-a-vid Henry, and he wan't doin' nothin' but just standin' there lookin' at the pond . . . and when I come back agin if there wan't Da-a-vid Henry standin' there just as if he's been there all day, gazin' down into that pond, and I says, "Da-a-vid Henry, what air you a-doin'?" And he didn't turn his head, but kept on lookin' down into that pond, and he said, as if he was thinkin' about the stars in the heavens, "Mr. Murray, I'm a-studyin' the habits of the bullfrog!" And there that darned fool had been standin' the live-long day— a-studyin'—the habits—of the bullfrog!

Thoreau stood still "the live-long day—a-studyin'." He was studying first-hand the habits of the bullfrog and the secrets of nature; and thousands of people today are happier for his activities in the field of "outdoor culture." His activity is recognized as being forward toward the goal of human enlightenment. The Black Queen ran herself into exhaustion and admitted she remained in the same place. Thoreau stood still and made progress.

The Black Queen represents the modern mechanistic cult—the worship of motion and transport for its own sake. Her activity is "lateral," not forward; she makes "transport" but not progress; we cannot call her a "transcendentalist," but we might with precise analogy call her a "transportationalist."

The activity of transportation and mechanization is a marvelous thing—but only when under control and kept in its proper place. This is in industry, not in culture or recreation. The objectives of industry are sublime—to provide the wherewithal for culture. We must develop the mechanistic phase of our civilization—but only as servant, never as master: we must never allow it to impair the primeval phase of our civilization—that environment of a full-bloomed, pristine nature which is the final source of all culture and enlightenment. A complete and balanced civilization requires both of these phases—the primeval and the mechanistic.

The city is the end product and cross-section of a *mechanical civilization*. It is more than this: it is the efflorescence of a total human civilization—both in industry and culture. It contains the waterfront and the railway terminal; and it contains the art gallery, the university, and the theatre. It is a focus of the high and low in human society —a measure of the tide "in the affairs of men." It is a marvelous product of the evolution of mankind. The forest on the other hand is the end product and efflorescence of a *primeval civilization* (for every forester knows that the primeval forest is an organized society). It is a product of the evolution of mankind's foundation. And so the forest is the root of man's society as the city is its head and flower. A civilization without its city would be a headless one; and a civilization without its forest is a rootless one. The forest alone without the city is the creator of the cave man; the city alone without the forest is the creator of the iron man.

Forest and city must grow side by side in any balanced civilization. When Sir James Bryce was ambassador to this country from England he made a speech in Washington in which he pointed out our capital city as one which appeared to be harbored in a forest. He referred, of course, to the shade trees which at that time so plentifully lined the city's streets. Because of these the view from the top of the Washington Monument presented a floral picture rather than a structural one. But shade trees are only the trimmings of the primeval environment. The forest as an entity must be woven within the matrix of our territorial development. Our early settlers first planted civilization by inroads of population through the forest; we today, in order to restore civilization, must develop forest inroads between our population centers. Only in this way can we effectively carry out the thought expressed by Mr. L. F. Kneipp of making "the forest a part of the life of the American people."

It is these "forest inroads" which, to my mind, should form the basis for any recreation plan for New England. They should form a series of embankments, or "levees," for controlling the flood of mechanistic civilization which is pouring forth, in the shape of temporal chaotic structures, along the motor ways outward from our metropolitan centers. This "flood" is getting out of hand. It is a notorious fact that the mechanistic phase of our society is, whether consciously or not, tending to run away with the whole of our society. It is stampeding society—just as the Black Queen stampeded little Alice. It is exhausting the energies of our society by moving our bodies and effects in a pointless, lateral movement over the face of the earth while leaving us in soul "just where we were before."

Physically speaking the laying out of these forest embankments should form no very complex problem in regional planning. In general they should follow the main mountain ranges, the steep-sided river canyons, secluded river bottoms, and other belts and corners of land where soil and topography are better suited to the growth of forest than to agricultural crops. They should follow the line of the Berkshires, the Green Mountains, the White Mountains, and the backbone of New Hampshire, the north woods of Maine, the Deerfield, the Naugatuck, and the other canyons of the central peneplain, and such miniature glacial scenery as the Pine Barrens of Cape Cod. These belts may be called "wilderness ways" (linear extensions of the "wilderness areas" suggested by Mr. Aldo Leopold); they should form a framework of public parks and forests connected by a series of paths or primitive trails equipped with cabins and facilities for camping and general outdoor living. Such a system of wilderness ways, when developed, would form the setting for the primal phase of New England's civilization, interlocking with the mechanical phase exhibited in the metropolitan centers and highways. As shade trees are to the city, so these wilderness ways would be to mechanical civilization generally. Forest and city in New England would grow side by side.

But the real basis for developing, in New England or in any other region, the proper setting and environment for the activity of outdoor recreation and of the pursuit of culture at its sources, is more than physical—it is psychologic. It consists in the creation or development of a genuine human interest, within a critical group or margin of the people, in the movement forward toward the infinite goals of evolution in place of a temporal human infatuation with lateral motion and mechanical transport for its own sake. It is the development of evolutionists as against "transportationalists." And this development is under way. It is the American outdoor movement. Its equivalent in Europe is known as the youth movement. It consists of the inevitable and irresistible impulse of humanity to right the balance of its civilization. It is a movement to uphold the primal phase of human life by a visioning of evolution on the out-of-doors horizon. It is the reposeful dynamics of "Da-a-vid Henry" versus the stampeding statics of the Black Queen.

Unprovided with this impulse, your public parks and forests and wilderness ways are a country without a prophet. And the impulse alone unprovided with its primal setting is a prophet without a country. It is the union of these two—of setting with activity—of the American forest with the American outdoor movement, which seems to be required in any real scheme for outdoor recreation. This is not my scheme, nor the scheme of any man, but it seems to be the scheme of nature. To develop this union in a definite series of wilderness ways, strategically located to control the streams of metropolitan flow—this to my mind is the fundamental policy behind any effective plan for recreation in New England. And only through this union, I believe, can we make of New England a land where we shall be content not merely to exist in fruitless motion but to *live* in the open field of evolution.

13.

Outdoor Culture
—The Philosophy
of Through Trails*

This term—"outdoor culture"—I am taking from Mr.
Chauncey J. Hamlin, of Buffalo, N. Y.** It is with a fear
and a tremble that I use the word "culture" because few
words have excited greater levity. However, I shall stand
by it, and shall endeavor to define it. By "culture" I mean
a special thing. It is not transcendentalism; it is not erudi-
tion; it is not necessarily "cultivated." It is a special kind of
ability: the ability to visualize a happier state of affairs
than the average humdrum of the regulation world. But in
order to make the matter clearer I shall use a worse term
yet: "Utopia."

Lewis Mumford has written a book called *The Story of
Utopias: the Other Half of the Story of Mankind*. In this
he defines two kinds: (1) the Utopia of reconstruction;
(2) the Utopia of escape.

Another name for Utopia is "pipe dream."

Reprinted from *Landscape Architecture,* Vol. XVII, No. 3
(April, 1927), pp. 163-71.
* Address given before New England Trail Conference, Boston,
January 21, 1927.

** Mr. Hamlin coined this term at a meeting in 1925, in Washington, of the President's Conference on Outdoor Recreation.

Magellan had a pipe dream when he visualized his voyage around the world. DeLesseps had a pipe dream when he visualized the Panama Canal. Samuel Piermont Langley had a pipe dream when he visualized the aeroplane. Each of these men visualized not a place but a world—a new mode of life. Each man in his own mind created a little world which eventually came to pass in the minds of other men. Here is one kind of pipe dream.

I can illustrate the other kind by a personal experience. I once saw Douglas Fairbanks in the photoplay *Robin Hood*. The hero climbs the proverbial tower; with one arm he catches the beautiful lady as she jumps to elude the bad man's attentions; with the other he continues climbing; then deftly annihilating Mr. Bad Man, he receives embraces nobly won. It was a glorious show. Intensely I imbibed it from start to finish, transferring my personality totally and thoroughly into Douglas's rugged body. For fifty cents I had been a hero for twice as many minutes. I left the theatre victorious, vicarious, and with my money's worth. Into this vivid little Utopia I had made my "getaway" from the humdrum of ordinary prosy life.

Here, then, are the two brands: the Utopia of creative thought, and the Utopia of effortless escape; the pipe dream of a Magellan, and that of a movie-fan; the real and the vicarious; the active and the imbibing. Which in the long run is the most fun? Foolish question, you say, because Mr. Average Man cannot be a Magellan. But wait! Why not? Certainly he can. Not a great one but a small one. It is *not* a foolish question.

Then let us look into it. Which would you rather be— a makebelieve Robin Hood, or a real (though diminutive) Magellan? We can be the first for fifty cents; what are the chances for becoming the second? How can we visualize our own little Utopia of creative thought and translate it into action? Well, in a hundred different ways. We shall consider only one: the constructive Utopia of "outdoor culture."

Outdoor culture is related to regional planning. That is why I am interested in it: because I would be a regional planner. Outdoor culture is to regional planning what amateur is to technician. If the technician is the brain, the amateur is the body and the soul. Outdoor culture is the soul and body of regional planning.

The regional planner, like the architect and the engineer, is a visualizer. His plan is a picture—a picture of possibilities. A civil engineer is given the job, let us say, of laying out a railway line across the divide of the Cascade Mountains. He makes a survey of the region's topography. From this he makes an accurate picture of what seems to be the most efficient line and grade for crossing the divide. He does not "plan" this line, he *finds* it. The line itself is a potentiality of nature's. Whatever "plan" there is has been made by forces higher than mere man. Man's greatness lies in *revealing* what this plan may be. Planning is revelation.

The regional planner, of course, deals very largely with industry: specifically he deals with the geographic layout of industrial plant. (But industry as a means and not an end in itself.) With the aid of the civil engineer he visualizes railway lines and possible waterpower projects; with the aid of the forester he visualizes the possibilities of replacing gradually a system of forest mining by a system of forest culture; with the aid of the agriculturist he visualizes the possibilities of remodelling the location of the various crops; with the aid of the industrial engineer he visualizes the gradual relocation, for the better, of the manufacturing industry and plant. Finally he tries to visualize an integration of this great labyrinth whereby we all shall be provided, via the most direct and efficient lines, with food, clothing, and shelter. Thus may we evolve (so far as geographic problems go) an efficient and labor-saving method of existing on our planet.

Existing! How about living? Man *lives* not by bread alone—nor by clothing, nor by shelter. What else (in geographic terms) is required for real "living" on our Earth? There is one more big category that needs to be provided. It is a material category and also a spiritual one: it is an extension of the category which we call "shelter." Each one of us, each family of us, needs a roof, and warmth, and light, and water supply, and some degree of plumbing. But it takes more than these to make a home. Each group of us who live in the same town needs houses and stores and streets and churches and school buildings: but it takes more than these to make a real community. The Nation of us needs towns and roads and industries and a host of other material plants, but it takes more than these to make a pleasant land to live in. Mere "shelter," therefore, will not suffice. We need a further category: it is part geography and part folks; it is terrestrial and it is human; it goes by the name *environment*.

Environment is outward influence: it is defined in the scientific books as the sum total of factors affecting an organism from *without*. Perhaps you will say that the outer world is less important than the inner mind. Thus apparently are we coming more and more to think in these days of psychology and radio and wave lengths. But what is the outer world except an extension of the inner mind? Is it not the life which all inner lives share? Environment indeed is a sort of *common mind*—the least common denominator of our inner lives.

The essence, therefore, of a pleasing environment is the thing that we call harmony: that which is agreeable to all our inner minds. The nearest approach to complete harmony seems to be achieved by the face of nature unaffected by mankind. Nature alone pleases a greater range of minds than nature modified by man. Where man comes in there discord is at hand.

> "Where every prospect pleases
> And only man is vile."

How may man's works upon Earth's surface be rendered more pleasing and less vile? How can they be made harmonious? The answer to this question is the ultimate quest of regional planning—and of its ally, outdoor culture. Harmony is balance. And balance, as Mr. Aldo Leopold puts it, is the sum and substance of planning. Surely this is so with matters of industrial layout. Unless so much forest goes with so much cattle range and so much corn land, then the country will get sick. Unless so much manufacturing goes with so much lumbering—and farming—and mining—then it will also get sick. And the country usually is ailing—just as we humans get to ailing when we eat too much starch and too few vitamines. And as with stomachs—and industries—so with environment: its health depends on balance.

Lack of balance results from lack of control. This applies to a whiskey drinker uncontrolled or to a civilization uncontrolled. As one tendency of a drinker is to overdrink, so one tendency of a civilization is to over-civilize. The artificial attempts to lord it over the natural. This is illustrated strikingly by the modern American city. For a city is a focus of civilization. In its growth and movements may be seen, in sharp relief, the dominant tendencies of the society it represents. In what direction is the modern American city moving?

The city's outward movements may be likened to a

glacier. It is spreading, unthinking, ruthless. In the original region of its expansion there would be, normally, several well defined communities, each one a distinct unit of humanity with its own tradition, government, and "personality." There is ready interchange with the other communities so that together they form the essence of a little "state." Then the "glacier" begins to flow. The original communities are one by one submerged. They are welded in a common suburban mass without form and without articulation: the integrity of each former human unit is ironed away; its local government is merged in general administration; its "personality" evaporates. Having swamped the immediate territory (and its little "state") the glacier flows on in radiating finger-shaped projections along the main highways. These projections, narrowing into tentacles, continue their inroads, via motor way and Socony station, toward the heart of the hinterland. As our country in geologic times underwent a glacial invasion, so to-day it is invested by a *metropolitan invasion*.

The modern metropolis is the product, not of its immediate region, but of the continent and of the world. It is a nerve center in a world-wide industrial system. Less and less is it indigenous; more and more is it a standardized exotic. It depends on tentacles rather than on roots. The effect of an unbalanced industrial life, it is the cause of an unbalanced recreational life. For its hectic influence widens the breach between normal work and play by segregating the worst elements in each. It divorces them into drubbing mechanized toil on the one hand and into a species of "lollipopedness" on the other.

Half of this picture—that of mechanized toil—has been depicted in some striking modern plays. The play *R. U. R.* shows the artificial laborer, all body and no brain. Another play, *The Adding Machine,* shows the mechanized clerk. But the other half of the picture will not be made complete till some great playwright comes along and writes *The Jelly Fish*.

You say I exaggerate. I do—deliberately. I want to bring out tendencies and ultimates. We are not as bad as this yet. But if we have not attained unto the "adding machine" we are fast approaching the "jelly fish." For even our society ladies now find themselves *"So tired!"* after a day in the city that by night they need complete and gelatinous "relaxation."

I might here wax eloquent and point out the warning of ancient Rome. Then I might borrow a term from Brook Farm and describe the "Civilizee." From all accounts Rome must have been getting on toward the ultimate of over-civilization. But she was lucky: for she had the Barbarian at her back gate.

And now I am nearing the point of the philosophy of through trails. It relates to the development of a certain type of modern (or future) American. It is the opposite type from the Civilizee. As Roman civilization received ultimately its cleansing invasion from the hinterland, so American civilization may yet receive its modern counterpart.

What manner of man may be the coming American "Barbarian"? A purifier? Yes, perhaps, but not a Puritan. The Barbarian which I have in mind is a rough and ready engineer. He understands water pressure and he understands human pressure. He knows that each demands its outlet. You cannot dam up *all* the water. Water at high level forms a high potential pressure, and the result of its release depends upon the sluiceway. If this be intact the flow becomes controlled and its power made constructive; if weak and leaky the power peters out or spreads disaster. As with water pressure so with soul pressure: its

"hydraulics" are the same. The Puritan would build
a dam; but the Barbarian would build a sluiceway.

Let us compare our Barbarian with our Civilizee. Each
is a tendency—an ultimate: perhaps no specimen of either
character has yet been born, but the embryos of both are
plain to see. Each has his own Utopia. Our Civilizee is
content to be a vicarious Robin Hood. Our Barbarian demands to be a real (if diminutive) Magellan—a pioneer
in the new exploration of a Barbarian Utopia. Our
Civilizee is content with the throb of the jazz band; our
Barbarian demands the ring and rhythm of the Anvil
Chorus. One is content with exotic metropolitan splendor;
the other prefers indigenous colonial color. The one sees
in colonial revival merely the worship of our grandfa-
thers; the other sees in it a future potential art to be developed by our grandsons. Our Civilizee sees in the mountain summit a pretty place on which to play at tin-can
pirate and to strew the Sunday supplement; our Barbarian
sees in the mountain summit the strategic point from
which to resoundly kick said Civilizee and to open war
on the further encroachment of his mechanized Utopia.

And now I come straight to the point of the philosophy
of through trails. *It is to organize a Barbarian invasion.*
It is a counter movement to the Metropolitan invasion.
Who are these modern Barbarians? Why, we are—the
members of the New England Trail Conference. As the
Civilizees are working outward from the urban centers we
Barbarians must be working downward from the mountain tops. The backbone of our strategy (in the populous
eastern United States) lies on the crestline of the Appalachian Range, the hinterland of the modern "Romes"
along the Atlantic coast. This crestline should be captured
—and no time lost about it.

The Appalachian Range should be placed in public

hands and become the site for a Barbarian Utopia. It matters little whether the various sections be State lands or Federal, or whether you spell them "Park" or "Forest" (with a capital F). The main thing is to capture these areas and to hold them from further inroads of metropolitanism. Aldo Leopold would call them "wilderness areas." They should be public lands and dedicated to a future American Barbarianism. But we should not wait upon legal transfer. Many of the present owners are with us now, for they are our fellow-Barbarians and they will help us. They have long since begun to help us by letting us cut trails upon their lands. So we need not delay. The through trails already established should be put still further *through*.

But this is not all. Cabins and trails are but a line of forts. We must get together our fighting force: we must mobilize our real (if diminutive) Magellans—our pioneers of a new exploration; we must visualize our Barbarian Utopia by developing our indigenous environment. We must do it thoroughly. We should survey and chart our *areas* of highland wilderness as well as cut our *lines* of trail. We should plot the boundaries of our realm. We should find and know what lies within—what forests, actual and potential; what upland range lands; what cabin sites; what vistas to unfold. And on this basis we should visualize a plan of occupation: that is, we should *reveal* the hidden plan of nature to this end.

And more: The main trails through these highland areas should be joined by "approach trails" from the lowlands. For we need branches and ramifications—that is, if we would make a *thorough* invasion. These approach trails should lead out from the hamlets. We have in these hamlets that other half of the indigenous environment— namely the colonial New England village. The colonial as well as the primeval environment should ultimately come within our realm. They are the two halves of the "indigenous." If our Barbarian invasion is to be complete, the colonial environment of the New England village must be captured and held from the Civilizees as well as the primeval environment of the mountains.

Such is our pipedream. Let Civilizees sleep on, content in their "Utopia of escape"; but let us Barbarians develop our Utopia of creative thought and action. Here in a word is the job of outdoor culture.

It happens that I have had the opportunity during the past autumn of taking some small steps in working out some of the "ramifications" just referred to. I have been working on the Wapack Trail with two of its chief promoters, Mr. William F. Robbins and Miss Marion H. Buck. The Bridgman School for Boys, located in the New England hamlet of Shirley Center, Massachusetts, has also taken up the work. A group of boys from this School, working under my direction, has put through the "Bridgman School Circuit over Kidder Mountain" as a branch of the Wapack Trail. The same group has also started an approach trail leading from the Bridgman School yard, in Shirley Center, via back roads and woodways, toward Watatic Mountain, there to join the Wapack Trail and tie into the general trail system.

Well, you have asked for a philosophy and I have tried to give you one. It is "outdoor culture"—the visualization of a particular Utopia of action. This consists in developing the indigenous environment (primeval and colonial) whereby the balance may tend to be restored between the natural and the artificial in our countryside and in our mode of living. It is a quest for harmony—for what is pleasing and not "vile" in that outward world which is our common mind. This philosophy—or culture—is, to my mind, the *raison d'être* of the through trail and its ramifications. It is "the why" of the Appalachian Trail, which—let us hope—may some day form the base for the strategy of a "Barbarian invasion," and for the development of a Barbarian Utopia.

Index

Wildlife protection: international, 91
Wildlife Treaty of Pan-American Union, 91
Wilson, Woodrow, 88
Wood, Franklin P., 40
Wright, Henry, 39

Yard, Robert Sterling: a founder of Wilderness Society, 38

Zahniser, Howard, 38
Zon, Raphael, 34-35, 79